C000051287

Project Ethics

For Ugla Huld and Andri Snær

Project Ethics

HAUKUR INGI JONASSON
and
HELGI THOR INGASON

GOWER

© Haukur Ingi Jonasson and Helgi Thor Ingason 2013

All rights reserved. No part of this publication may be reproduced, stored in a retrieval system or transmitted in any form or by any means, electronic, mechanical, photocopying, recording or otherwise, without the prior permission of the publisher.

Published by
Gower Publishing Limited
Wey Court East
Union Road
Farnham
Surrey, GU9 7PT
England

Gower Publishing Company
110 Cherry Street
Suite 3-1
Burlington
VT 05401-3818
USA

www.gowerpublishing.com

Haukur Ingi Jonasson and Helgi Thor Ingason have asserted their moral rights under the Copyright, Designs and Patents Act, 1988, to be identified as the authors of this work.

British Library Cataloguing in Publication Data
Jonasson, Haukur Ingi.
  Project ethics. -- (Advances in project management)
  1. Project management--Moral and ethical aspects.
  I. Title II. Series III. Ingason, Helgi Thor.
  658.4'04-dc23

ISBN: 978-1-4094-1096-6 (pbk)
ISBN: 978-1-4094-1097-3 (ebk – PDF)
ISBN: 978-1-4094-8452-3 (ebk – ePUB)

Library of Congress Cataloging-in-Publication Data
Haukur Ingi Jsnasson.
  Project ethics / by Haukur Ingi Jonasson and Helgi Thor Ingason.
    p. cm. -- (Advances in project management)
  Includes bibliographical references and index.
  ISBN 978-1-4094-1096-6 (hbk) -- ISBN 978-1-4094-1097-3
  (ebook) -- ISBN 978-1-4094-8452-3 (epub) 1. Project management--Moral and ethical aspects. I. Ingason, Helgi Thor. II. Title.
  HD69.P75.H3784 2013
  174'.4--dc23

                                                              2012037708

Printed and bound in Great Britain by the MPG Books Group, UK

CONTENTS

LIST OF FIGURES

ABOUT THE AUTHORS

Haukur Ingi Jonasson (Cand. theol., University of Iceland; STM, MPhil, PhD, Union Theological Seminary (Columbia University); clinical training in pastoral counselling, Lennox Hill Hospital; psychoanalytical training, Harlem Family Institute New York City) is an assistant professor at the Reykjavik University School of Science and Engineering. He heads the MPM (Master in Project Management) programme at the University. He is a psychoanalyst in private practice and a management consultant at Nordica Consulting Group (Iceland). As a consultant, his clients have included the Icelandic National Energy Authority, major Icelandic banks, the University Hospital of Iceland, and other public and private organisations. Dr Jonasson is also a mountain climber and a member of the Reykjavik Air Ground Search and Rescue Squad.

Helgi Thor Ingason (PhD in process metallurgy, Norwegian Institute of Technology; MSc in mechanical and industrial engineering, University of Iceland; SCPM degree, Stanford University) is an associate professor at the Reykjavik University School of Science and Engineering and lectures in project management, quality management and facility planning. He heads the MPM (Master in Project Management) programme at the University. He is an IPMA certified senior project manager; a co-founder and senior consultant at Nordica Consulting Group (Iceland); and is co-founder and board member of Alur, alvinnsla hf – a recycling company in the Icelandic aluminium industry. In 2010–2011, he served as interim CEO of Orkuveita Reykjavikur (Reykjavik Energy). In his spare time Dr Ingason plays the piano and accordion with the South River Band (www.southriverband.com), an Icelandic world music ensemble.

ACKNOWLEDGEMENTS

We have wanted to write a book on project ethics for many years because we have seen, both as academics teaching various aspects of project, quality and corporate management, and as management consultants, a dissonance between managerial practice and the intellectual tradition which deals with sound, authentic decision-making and self-actualisation: ethics.

When two of our students, Hildur Helgadóttir MPM and Sigurður Fjalar Sigurðarson MSc, took a special interest in the field of project ethics, we decided that the time had come to sit down and get some writing done. We would like to thank them for their interest and enthusiasm. We especially want to thank Sigurður for his support and dedication to this project and for allowing us to pepper it with his MSc research. Without his enthusiasm, this book might not have come into existence.

Further, we want to thank all of our MPM students, and all of the project management professionals who took the time to answer the survey that was sent out by Sigurður Fjalar Sigurðarson. This gave us a lot of information that was truly invaluable. Hildur's paper 'The Ethical Dimension in Project Management' was published in the *International Journal of Project Management*, 2008 (Helgadóttir, 2008).

We want to thank Angela Sullivan, Steve Flinders and Bob Dignen at York Associates for reading over the book proposal, and Jane Appleton, Jón Ásgeir Sigurvinsson, Emily Lethbridge, Barni Randver Sigurvinsson and Nick Brieger for reading over the manuscript and for giving invaluable suggestions. We would also like to express our appreciation to Anouk Petzold Aoun, Marie Françoise Aoun, Carol Reid and Jean-François Gaillard for their support. Special thanks go to Darren Dalcher, who initiated the publishing project and put us in touch with Gower Publishing and encouraged us to write the book. Then we would like to thank our colleagues at the University of Iceland and University of Reykjavik and the Laboratory of Innovation and Energy Reclamation at the Albert Nerken School of Engineering at the Cooper Union in New York and its Director, Robert Dell. Very Special thanks go to Tim Morrissey and Alistair Godbold for their great input into the book in the final phase and to Jonathan Norman, Kevin Selmes, Melissa Young, Fiona Martin, Nicky Staskiewicz, Diane Thompson and everyone else at Gower Publishing for their support, suggestions and patience.

Then we would like to thank our colleagues and friends who teach with us on the Masters in Project Management (MPM) programme at the University of Reykjavik for endless stimulating conversations: Pall Jensson; Gudfinna Bjarnadottir; Runolfur Smari Sigthorsson; Benedikt Arnason; Asbjorg Kristinsdottir; Haraldur Flosi Tryggvason; Throstur Gudmundsson; Adalheidur Sigurdardottir; Margret Palsdottir; Thordur Vikingur Fridgeirsson; Hlynur Stefansson; Sæunn Kjartansdottir; Bjorg Sveinsdottir and all the other Icelanders who work with us; Steven D. Eppinger, General Motors LGO Professor of Management at Sloan School of Management at MIT; Morten Fangel, Hans J. Thamhain Professor of Management at Bentley University; Mark Morgan, Chief Executive Advisor at StratEx Advisors and Lecturer on the Stanford SAPM programme; and Markus Zoller, owner and CEO of Zompec AG. In addition, we would like to thank the inspiring participants at the annual IPMA expert seminars in Zurich, and other interesting people we have come across at IPMA conferences, including Hans Knöpfel, Miles Shepard, David L. Pells at PMForum (www.pmforum.org), and Rodney Turner, editor of the *International Journal of Project Management*.

INTRODUCTION

PROJECT ETHICS

The aim of this book is to shine a light on the neglected area of *project ethics* in project management with practising project leaders and managers as the main target audience. We will explore project ethics using a set of practical decision-making tools to navigate around problems by reference to a value system that incorporates our human nature and our motivations in the broadest sense. The text includes a discussion on the nature of ethics, provides a series of practical examples to illustrate the range of grey-area problems and how to present dilemmas that may be encountered in project management, and suggests how these can be approached. This book is international in its scope. However, it uses a few illustrations from Iceland, owing to the authors' greater familiarity with events there, and the belief that these provide a prism through which the relevant concepts can be understood more readily.

The project leader is a key player in many of the most important endeavours that modern societies undertake, and often in a tough environment where values, people's rights, cultural and natural treasures are all too easily neglected in the pursuit of monetary rewards.

The field of project management is diverse and readers of this book will have a wide spectrum of interests, coming at it from many different angles. Your view of how ethics affects your decision-making role may naturally vary, depending on your answers to the following questions:

- Are you part of a for-profit or a not-for-profit enterprise?
- Are you a project sponsor, initiator and owner?
- Are you an employee/contractor hired to implement other people's plans?
- Do you operate in a legal, supervisory or regulatory role?
- Are your interests tied to the early delivery or eventual profitability of a project? Or are you paid the same, regardless of the outcome?
- Is your role rigidly defined or does it allow for some latitude in decision-making?

- Are you at the earlier or later stages of your career?
- Do you take a short-term or long-term outlook in relation to your role?

Your ethical perspective may also be coloured by the role you play, with some aspects considered more or less important than others. However, this does not change the underlying nature of ethics. Ethical theories and how they relate to decision-making are independent concepts that have been gradually introduced and have subsequently evolved over millennia, with the earliest documentation of ethics beginning with the ancient Greeks, some 2,500 years ago.

Since antiquity, human beings have worked at both the individual and collective level to realise their aspirations by planning and executing projects, ranging from the small and simple to the large and complex. While many aspects of project management and delivery have evolved considerably, others have changed little over time. These aspects can be considered as being universal in nature, and it is important to be aware of them throughout the life cycle of a project from initial conception through to the execution and outcome stages.

In many cases, projects have straightforward origins that may or may not evolve into something far more complex. For example, the age-old problem of how we transport X under conditions Y from A to B can cover everything from the installation of an irrigation system to the landing of a man on the moon. Another example could be how we make Z return by providing the means of money exchange between Group C, who are savers, and Group D, who are borrowers. This can cover everything from plain vanilla banking to the design of highly complex financial derivative products. The first question that will arise in all cases is whether or not the reason for the project stands up to moral scrutiny and this is naturally a very subjective area. It will, further, depend on many considerations such as the expected rate of return on the investment, the time horizon of the project and the degree of socio-environmental interaction and impact.

After the initial origination phase, project leaders can be faced with difficult choices regarding projects. How to select a project? How to plan a project? How to execute a project? How to finalise the project? Should we choose Option A or B when Option A will deliver the project on time and budget but we will have to compromise our perception of what is right and wrong in the process, and vice versa for Option B?

As projects become larger, the potential for conflict in both the execution and outcome of a project inevitably increases and project initiators of all sorts – investors, policy makers, sponsors, project leaders, members of project teams – are likely to face a broad range of problems in this regard. Some of these problems will be largely technical (designing an engine, building a bridge), while others will be largely non-technical (planning a festival, implementing democratic processes), requiring alternative approaches. In all projects (technical or non-technical), there may be difficult personal issues, political problems, and general conflicts arising where there are competing values at stake; for example, human rights vs. profit, health and safety vs. output, respect vs. productivity. In these instances, the problems can often become ethical ones, requiring reflection on individual or communal core values, and considerations such as long-term reputation may become increasingly important.

When we ask our colleagues, students and clients to give us examples of ethical management problems, they usually come up with ideas involving bribery, theft, dishonesty, sexual harassment, employee security and stakeholder rights. What we find interesting is how narrowly this domain seems to be defined. Therefore, what we aim to convey in this book is that the scope of issues of ethical significance that management needs to tackle is much broader than has usually been considered.

While there has been a great deal of academic work carried out on the nature of project successes since the 1950s and many interesting new ideas and managerial tools have been developed, when it comes to ethical and moral deliberation around projects, the project management literature is somewhat sparse and inadequate. Unfortunately, ethics has been restricted to rather limited aspects of managerial practice while, in reality, it should be considered to be a constant and limitless concept that should infuse, inspire, instigate and influence all of what we think and do as a professional. Competence in ethical analysis, reflection and decision-making should *not* be seen as a secondary ability, but as an integral skill of the project leader to advance along the path of sustainable and mature practice.

BOOK OVERVIEW

In this introduction to the emerging field of *project ethics* we will show how ethics can be used for propagating professionalism within the field of project management and how it can become a powerful tool to identify opportunities and risks in project-leader practice. The book aims to provide serious and detailed answers to the following three questions:

- How should project management scholars and practitioners understand project ethics?
- How relevant is ethics to project management?
- How can ethics be used as one of the most fundamental guides in the decision-making of future professional project leaders?

In Chapter 1, the book sets out to illustrate briefly the importance of ethics and to highlight the shortcomings in the current project management literature in relation to how to identify and deal with those problems that arise where a conflict of values exists between different entities during a project. The well-known project management concept of *critical path* is described and the possibility that there might be other critical pathways that project leaders should explore is discussed, with particular reference to the field of *philosophical ethics*. In order to demystify this field for project management professionals, general managers and project initiators alike, the topic is broken down into a series of concepts that are individually introduced. A brief introduction is given to ethical theories based on virtue, utility, duty and rights that can be used to evaluate projects and make sound decisions at all stages within the project life cycle.

We also discuss professional standards and ethical codes that the project management profession has defined and introduce a recent survey carried out among 220 up-to-date International Project Management Association (IPMA) certified[1] project leaders in Iceland to help understand the level of awareness of project ethics and its relevance amongst different sectors of the Icelandic economy.

In Chapters 2 to 5, the separate concepts relating to the different aspects of project ethics introduced in Chapter 1 are discussed in detail. Chapter 2 begins by looking at project management from the perspective of virtue. The focus here is on the project leader as an individual, his or her accomplishments and professional identity. In Chapter 3, we discuss the concept of utility and take a closer look at what has been regarded as critical success criteria in traditional project management. Here the focus is on the overall *outcome* of the project in terms of utility, and on utilitarian principles of ethics, success and development. In Chapter 4, we discuss duty and rules of conduct in terms of universal professional principles and explore how to create well-defined principles that should then be used to define the project *process*. In Chapter 5, we discuss the rights of different entities within the project *process*, and the concept of the social contract that balances the rights of different stakeholders is explained. In Chapter 6, we carry out a detailed synthesis of the material presented in the previous sections and discuss the basics of how to identify, evaluate and make decisions regarding ethical opportunities and risks in projects. This draws on the four main concepts that operate on five different levels throughout the project life cycle and forms the basis for the introduction of a new method. This method, based on classical ethical theory, can help project owners, project leaders, project teams and stakeholders to identify, evaluate and make ethically sound decisions. This tool demands ethical thinking from project leaders and invites them to view ethical aspects of their projects as success factors. The tool should promote ethical awareness and encourage project leaders to develop

---

1   International Project Management Association certification is a competence-based standard that provides a benchmark for recruitment, training and development of project and programme managers and project teams. More information, including the IPMA Competence Baseline, can be found on the IPMA website, www.impa.ch.

their own socially responsible and sustainable decision-making in future situations where conflicting values are apparent.

Throughout the book, a series of short case studies or vignettes are included from real project management examples from around the globe which aim to illustrate the ethical concepts that have been introduced. Additionally, a series of questions is periodically asked to encourage the reader to reflect on where competing values may surface in the course of a project, to assess the relevance of this phenomenon, and to think how successfully it can be dealt with using the conceptual framework put forward in this book as a guide.

Even though the book mainly focuses on project management, it might as well be a reference to programme and portfolio management in general. Affiliated with the book is the webpage of our consulting company Nordica Consluting Group – (www.ncg.is) and a new homepage where one can find the Project Ethics Tool (PET) (www.projectethics.is). We encourage our readers to visit these webpages; on the latter site one can find a tool to evaluate project risks.

CHAPTER 1

THE CRITICAL PATH OF PROJECT ETHICS

WHAT IS ETHICS?

Ethics can be defined as the discipline, often classified as a sub-discipline of philosophy, that is concerned with what is good and just for individuals, groups, organisations and society. The discipline investigates the nature of our well-being and happiness, the appropriate pathways to our prosperity, our obligations, and, related to all this, the rights that we owe to ourselves and to one another. In modern society, ethics defines how individuals, professionals, corporations and societies choose to interact with one another.

The word *ethics* comes from the Greek word *ethos* meaning 'character', and the discipline has been constantly developed through generations of philosophers, including Socrates, Plato, Aristotle, Plutarch, Cicero, Avicenna, and the Renaissance and modern philosophers. Ethics has to do with morality, but morality can be said to be a reality – norms, ideas, attitudes – that is just there for good or for bad, just like the communication systems that we employ in our day-to-day behaviour and in our language. Whether we like it or not, we all partake in the moral reality, by thinking about moral issues and making moral choices. We do so even when the choice is to avoid making any choice or being ignorant or apathetic on moral issues. Every time we think of what we did in the past, what we should be doing now, or what we should be doing in the future, we are thinking to some extent about our morality. Morality, however, is not ethics. If morality is the lived ethical domain, then ethics is the principled investigation of that domain.

Ethical guidelines are derived from experience and observation of the long-term wider consequences of actions. The field is constantly evolving as our technologies advance, and our collective wisdom grows as the facts surrounding negative events emerge over time. Outside scrutiny by fellow professionals and/or the wider public and the formation of a consensus opinion is often the final arbiter in these matters. For example, failing to abide by an ethical code of practice can be detrimental to the reputation of a professional and can seriously damage their career advancement and prospects.

A recent example is the phone hacking scandal in the UK that led to the overnight closure of the *News of The World* newspaper, which had been in existence since 1843, with sales of several million copies weekly. The critical factor in this was the unethical methods used to gather information and the cavalier way in which the families and friends of serious crime victims were treated. This overstepping of ethical boundaries was subsequently severely dealt with in the court of public opinion and it is likely that the repercussions of this scandal will continue to reverberate for some time yet, requiring a number of senior managers to defend their actions surrounding the whole affair. Other examples include companies such as Raytheon, BAe Systems, Siemens and Enron who have suffered reputational damage, impact to their business, sometimes to the point of collapse.

The recent banking collapse in Iceland is another example where unethical behaviour resulted in a negative outcome, in this case national bankruptcy. A comprehensive and damning 2,300 page report published in early 2010 by the Icelandic Truth Commission, headed by Icelandic Supreme Court Judge Páll Hreinsson, catalogued a whole range of unethical behaviour involving bankers, senior politicians and regulators. A complex web of cross-holdings and compromised lending decisions, involving the majority owners of the banks in question, was laid bare as well as a series of regulatory failures, which masked the reality that 'weak equity' accounted for 70 per cent of the banks' reported core capital. As a result, other investors were duped on a wholesale basis, and the international reputational repercussions from these events will cause problems for Iceland for many years to come.

These examples show what can happen when ethical boundaries are crossed and are exceptional cases rather than being indicative of normality. It is now the case that a comprehensive code of ethics is to be found at the heart of most modern professional fields with medical practitioners, engineers, accountants and project professionals in different jurisdictions each having their own tailored version. These codes are formed from a combination of general ethical theories and experience derived from within those fields. There are a number of situations within professional practice where ethics are particularly important and some of these are listed below:

- Where client confidentiality is of paramount importance.
- Where bad decision-making can have direct serious consequences for others.
- Where outcomes are difficult to measure and/or assign responsibility to and bad decision-makers can hide behind the consequent ambiguity.
- When negative outcomes only occur long after the initial acts have occurred and the people responsible have sufficient time to distance themselves from their bad decisions and actions.
- When concepts of fairness and justice in dealing with others are easily overlooked.

If, for example, you are one of a number of employees within a large organisation with access to a large amount of personal data relating to customers or clients, there may be a temptation, either through unintentional complacency or by deliberate design, to use this information for something other than its intended purpose. If done discreetly, it may be almost impossible to be caught doing this, and consequent negative outcomes for the person whose data was compromised may not be traceable to the original source. *But these cases occur nonetheless*, and this is a phenomenon that is not all that uncommon worldwide. In order to safeguard against this type of behaviour, a strong ethical culture from the top to the bottom of an organisation is essential, as well as vigilance on the part of other employees.

In the remaining sections of this chapter we will focus on current thinking in the field of project management, and discuss how project ethics has been dealt with in the project management literature to date. A number of basic ethical concepts will be introduced, as well as a review of some current ethical guidelines and a discussion about the results of a recent survey on the perception of ethics in the business community in Iceland.

THE DISCIPLINE OF PROJECT MANAGEMENT

Project management is a general term that covers a multitude of different roles across a range of sectors. The essential shared aspects of these roles are the willingness to take responsibility for delivering a set of outcomes, and the competence to organise and deliver those outcomes. The term can refer to either the management of individual projects, which tend to have defined time periods and aims, a programme which consists of more than one project having related aims, or a portfolio where there are a number of projects that will have unrelated or loosely related aims.

In modern times, project management has come to represent a unique discipline with its own special field of study, having emerged in the 1950s with the development of techniques like the Programme Evaluation and Review Technique (PERT) and the Critical Path Method (CPM). In particular, it has been influenced by the demands of industry and the military to establish, define, plan, schedule, execute and control complex projects. Ever since then, planning and scheduling, managing budgets and evaluating quality has been the main focus of project management practice, research and development. This is often displayed in conceptual form as the Iron Triangle, which has the aspects of time, cost and quality at each corner.

A crucial part of the development of project management as a discipline has been the way of thinking about project success. The questions that have been asked, and are still being asked, are:

- What is a successful project?
- What should be the success criteria in project management?
- What are the contributing factors to project success?
- What makes a successful project leader?
- What is project failure and what causes it?

Given its origins, it is evident that technical considerations have been given the highest priority in the project management literature and the three basic success criteria of the Iron Triangle (time, cost and quality) form the basis for the formal decision-making process. This approach, however, has been criticised for being inadequate for a variety of reasons by a number of authors (see, for example: Shenhar, Levy and Dvir, 1997; Shenhar, Dvir, Levy and Maltz, 2001; Atkinson, 1999; Baccarini, 1999; Pinto and Slevin, 1988). Atkinson (1999) defined project success both in terms of the Iron Triangle, that is, in regards to the *outcome*, and the project management success, that is, in regards to the *process*. Bryde (2005) admits that the conventional parameters of project success are constrained by the practical difficulties of assessing success using more subjective success criteria. These criteria could, for instance, be defined as the logical, ethical and/or aesthetic attributes of either the project process or the project outcome.

It has been assumed that better scheduling techniques would lead to greater project success and that if a project exceeded its due date or budget, or the outcome did not satisfy predetermined performance criteria, the project was assumed to be a failure (Belassi and Tukel, 1996). So far so good. However, something might be missing from this picture. Should the sense of virtue of the project leader, team, organisation, or society after they have accomplished their project be taken into account? What about other utility criteria and opportunity costs? What about whether things were done according to a vague or biased sense of duty? What if the project violates the rights of stakeholders or interested parties?

It is often said that success can be the greatest enemy of innovation. This is because it can lead to the perpetuation of false beliefs about what is actually required to achieve success; one can become blind to the importance of other factors if one relies on too narrow-minded an approach in the future. We will keep this in mind as we explore project success and speculate on how to link ethical theory to project practice. Could it be that in the attempt to define project success we are leaving out something essential development?

This book has two main objectives: one is to investigate how project success has been defined and measured within the project management field; the other, our main purpose, is to explain how project leaders can consider ethical factors as critical to upholding project management as a professional endeavour. Even though ethical considerations might often be difficult to measure in terms of either quantity or quality, we should not overlook measuring the things that we should be measuring, just because other things are more easily measurable. Ethics is also talked about in absolute terms: there is a single right and wrong. The very fact that it is a dilemma means that this single truth may not be the same for all stakeholder groups. Therefore, the decision and the reasons for it must be communicated clearly.

Project ethics is related to the concept of higher values in our awareness and dealings, and is guided by what is considered to be of benefit to society as a whole. This area is the main focus of this book but, if one went further, one could additionally invoke spirituality as a guide in our role as project leaders. In this case, spirituality is considered to be an inner path enabling a person to discover the essence of his or her being; or the deepest values and meanings by which people live. A ready example of project management guided in this fashion is evident in the works of missionaries of the world's major religions. Whether one agrees or not with the aims of their endeavours, it is undeniably the case that huge outcomes have been achieved with spirituality as the main guiding force. There is an argument to suggest that spirituality might help project leaders sustain meaning, culture and joy in their project teams. This topic is outside the scope of this book but is certainly worth exploring in greater detail.

THE CRITICAL PATH

The term *critical path* is among the most fundamental concepts in contemporary project management. It usually refers to a mathematically based algorithm that is used to schedule a set of project activities so as to optimise the use of time and resources (Kelly 1961). Defining the critical path is a standard practice in professional project management.

Owing to its importance, the critical path method has often been considered to be a symbolic milestone and a starting point for the establishment of modern project management as a formal discipline. Traditionally, project management has focused on the quality of the project outcome, and its time and cost. This has meant that in order to guarantee an acceptable outcome, the project leader would deploy a work breakdown structure – a well-defined list of all tasks that had to be completed within a project in order to reach the desired outcome. This took into account the understanding that certain tasks and a certain sequencing of tasks were more important than others for delivering the project within a given time. Identifying this critical path of tasks through the project became an important management tool and marks the origin of project management as a sub-discipline of operations research and engineering management.

However, this concept of a critical path, defined purely by considerations of quality, cost and time, may seem to be overly restrictive. As a result, someone coming from the disciplines of the humanities and social sciences might ask if there are any *other* types of critical paths in projects, in addition to time? If so, could these other paths be at least as critical as the system of tasks that are being connected along the project life cycle?

Recent trends suggest that other critical paths can be identified and, in the last decade or so, the project management community has focused a great deal on documenting the critical paths of good communication, good leadership and good understanding of how people think, behave, collaborate and operate. Indeed, topics like emotions in projects and sustainable project management seem to be gaining increased interest in the project management community. This is only natural, as the time has come for the profession to open its eyes more to the global community and to the wider world of psychological and social realities.

The International Project Management Association (IPMA), founded in 1965, the UK Association for Project Management (APM) founded in 1972 and the Project Management Institute (PMI), established in 1984, are organisations that oversee and promote the awarding of competence-based qualifications in project management. These qualifications provide a benchmark for the recruitment, training and development of project management staff and are recognised by businesses and organisations around the world. The aim of this book is to add to the current project management literature by elaborating on the subject of project ethics within the field of project management, and prompting and assisting the reader to answer the following questions:

- How well are project leaders aware of ethical success factors in their projects?
- Do project leaders truly measure the success of their projects in terms of time, cost, quality, and customer satisfaction?
- Do project leaders consider ethical factors in their projects and do they conduct ethical risk assessment?
- Is there a way to describe a simple framework that guides project leaders in evaluating ethical aspects of their projects and account for possible ethical risk?

The IPMA Competence Baseline Version 3 (ICB 3) is the basis for the IPMA 4 Level certification system and sets out the knowledge and experience expected from the managers of projects, programmes and project portfolios. It contains basic terms, practices, methods and tools for professional project management, as well as specialist knowledge and experience. The ICB 3 eye of competence shown in Figure 1.1 shows schematically the balance necessary to make a successful project leader, and this way of thinking can be a revelation to people who previously only considered technical competence to be of sole importance. The APM Body of Knowledge also makes explicit reference to ethics as a required competence for project professionals.

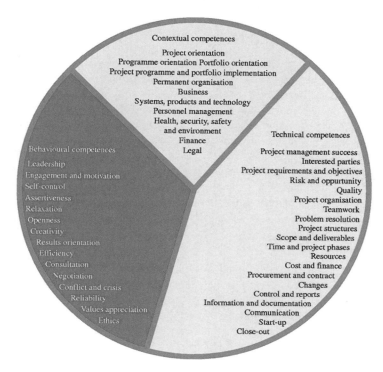

Figure 1.1   IPMA international competence baseline, eye of competence

In the same way that most of us strive to walk the critical path of good deeds throughout our lives, aiming for the greater good, pleasure, maturity and happiness, project leaders also have their own view of desirable critical paths where they can see that they have maintained appropriate conduct in their undertakings, and that they have done the right things in the right way. In saying this, it can be difficult for project leaders to avoid having to make difficult choices regarding projects, and some of the case studies included in this book refer to classic grey-area situations where there are no clear answers as to how to proceed.

Case 1 – Adam and Empower

Adam, an experienced project leader in an independent ISO14001[1] certified engineering consultancy firm, is asked to compile a report for the management of a major utility company outlining a number of different options for the size and location of a new power plant. The working title of the report is 'Empower'. Adam suspects that management already has a preconceived idea about what they desire; he is also sure that this would be controversial and vigorously opposed by other local stakeholders. These other local stakeholders argue that the demand projection figures upon which the project is based are over optimistic and that a solution involving a number of smaller plants built sequentially at different sites would be more appropriate/suitable.

Questions:

- How does this relate to ethics?
- What are the ethical considerations in the case?
- What are the competing values?
- What are Adam's options?

---

1   The ISO 14000 environmental management standards exist to help organisations (a) minimize how their operations (processes, and so on) negatively affect the environment (that is, cause adverse changes to air, water, or land); (b) comply with applicable laws, regulations, and other environmentally oriented requirements, and (c) continually improve in the above (www.wikipedia.org [accessed: 27 December 2011]).

What if, in order to deliver the project on time and on budget, we have to compromise our perception of what is right and wrong in the process? In this case, we might even compromise our sense of what professionalism entails, our responsibilities and/or sense of justice, and act in a way that opposes our moral standards. Alternatively, we might do the right thing according to our moral standards, but in doing so we would not deliver the project on time and on budget, or it might not generate the desired financial gain. In this case we might have to choose between the critical path in the traditional sense within project management and the critical path that we need to follow to actualise our personal moral values. How to make such decisions? This book proposes some tools and ways of thinking to help project leaders do so.

Research in project management has advanced in recent decades and the practical application of this research has provided the practitioners with useful new ideas, tools and methods. Practitioners can apply innovative ways to help measure and follow up on project success by using, for example, the balanced scorecard, critical success factors and the diamond approach. The emphasis in project management has naturally been on functionality, practicality, success, achievement and utility. We will, however, attempt to convince the reader that all of this has been coming from too limited a perspective, and to show that much has been left out concerning human conduct, actions and projects. In other words applied, ethics has yet to be incorporated into the official consensus on project success. We believe this omission is unfortunate as there are many fundamental principles and insights from moral theory and ethics that can guide investors, policy makers, project owners, project sponsors, project leaders and project teams in their endeavours. It is not enough to do what is right; if you are to be successful others must be convinced that it is right also.

PROJECT ETHICS

In modern terms *ethics* is the systematic and principled thinking of our moral conduct. *Project ethics* will be defined here as the moral deliberation and the self-actualisation processes that professional project management should require. A *narrow definition* of project ethics would be that it refers to a behavioural competence of project leaders that enables them to know when their professional identity might be compromised. A *broader definition* would claim that project ethics is not only one competence of many, but rather the core of what defines the project leader as a professional and, therefore, something that lies at the heart of the project management profession as such. Project ethics could also be viewed in terms of ethical opportunities and risks, and boils down to questions such as:

- Should we do it?
- Should we not?
- What exactly should we do?
- How should we do it?
- How should it be communicated?

One predominant idea of human nature in the Western intellectual tradition has been that people are driven primarily by self-serving needs, only caring about repercussions from their actions in a very limited sense. We see traces of this notion in theology, philosophy, biology, psychology and economics. This notion has also left its mark on applied sciences such as management and project management. In many fields, it is only in the last decades that we have started to see a genuine interest in exploring, scientifically, the individual interest in the well-being of others, which manifests itself, for instance, in creativity and altruism. The previous view of human nature as selfish and unconcerned with wider issues has been used to justify a certain detached ignorance and even an apathetic approach to business, engineering and to project management. This needs to be challenged.

The sceptical reader might ask: is project ethics, therefore, simply about moralising the project management discipline? The short answer is no. However, as we have seen above, ethics is concerned with the self-actualisation and successes of individuals, teams, organisations and societies, and takes into consideration the greater environment. What naturally derives from this is that project ethics is concerned with anything that has the status of a critical success factor in project management.

Ethical issues surface in all projects. In general, these issues can relate to the self-actualisation of the project leader; or they might have to do with the team; or they can be at an organisational level; or they might raise concerns from a societal perspective. More specifically, ethical questions might relate to the managerial methods used, demeanours, sponsorship, logistics, strategy, planning, execution, control, shares and stakeholder management. Different ethical issues can also arise at different stages of the project life cycle.

The project as a whole might also be ethically challenging. It might risk personal and/or organisational reputation; or it might be hazy in terms of estimates; or challenge our understanding of what it means to be a responsible citizen; and/or generate danger, burdens, or what economists call 'negative externalities' to innocent third parties, owing to incidental harm brought about by the project. The inability to critically identify, evaluate and manage ethical factors as a critical aspect of project management not only affects project success or failure in the traditional sense; it also undermines the profession and demoralises, weakens and destabilises societies. Taking a critical ethical perspective on success while preparing and executing a project plan is likely to be, therefore, time well spent.

Project ethics, as presented in this book, considers ethics on five levels: the individual, the team, the organisation, society and from the perspective of future generations. Ultimately, projects can fail, despite the planning and execution being well orchestrated, just because they are, or appear to be, ethically unsound on some level. What follows is intended to guide future project leaders to help them avoid such failures by moving beyond traditional notions of project success towards a more sustainable approach of collective project development.

HOW ETHICS IS NOT 'JUST ETHICS'

It is common to differentiate between descriptive ethics and normative ethics. *Descriptive ethics* aims to define and depict ethical situations, norms and behaviour; *normative ethics* aims to provide guiding principles and tools for better decision-making. Note that we say 'better decision-making', not 'better *ethical* decision-making'. The reason for this is that we see ethical decision-making not as something that is a side-track in general project decision-making, but as something that lies at the core of all project management assessment.

Project ethics, therefore, should not be seen as 'just ethics', meaning a discipline that can be left solely to the philosophers to debate and speculate about, but rather as a fundamental determination for the project management practitioner. To claim that ethics is not 'just ethics' might strike philosophically oriented readers as a fatal contradiction in terms. What is meant in this case is that project leaders usually have a set of 'hard' success criteria when managing their projects and then, on top of this, or alongside this, there may be ethical considerations. This is the mistake. Project ethics is not something that can or should be considered as just one of the competences at the project leader's disposal. Project ethics is rather the core of what defines the project leader as a professional, and normative ethics can, furthermore, provide project leaders with the most important decision-making tools they can possess.

Why is this so? We should be able to justify all our actions with reasons, and unethical behaviour or morally unsound decision-making in project management can drastically impact on project success. This has been discussed to a certain extent in the project management literature. Nicoló (1996) came up with the total ethical risk analysis (TERA) method that aids project leaders in decision-making by having them consider various ethical risks in projects. Examples of potential risks are moral and social harms, negative feedback from users and subsequent legal and economic risks, and risk that comes from distrust. One of the key points made by Nicoló is that 'dealing with applied ethics requires the adoption of both a particular anthropological model and specific theoretical foundations of normative ethics'.

Loo (2002) has a multi-dimensional outlook on ethical dilemmas and moral decision-making in project management. He uses vignettes, or short narratives, that embody ethical dilemmas in project planning, execution and termination. The vignettes are analysed using Reidenbach and Robins' (1990) 30-item ethical response scale, and mirrored in five categories of normative ethics: justice, relativism, egoism, utilitarianism and deontology. We share Loo's belief that vignettes – or short descriptive stories that explain an ethical dilemma – are a useful way to present ethical dilemmas and get a response. Therefore, we frequently refer to vignettes as case studies in this book. We also note, however, that our interpretation of what aspects of a project require ethical consideration is somewhat wider than Loo's.

Meredith and Mantel (2005) discuss ethics in relation to topics such as the request for proposals process, public safety, and the environment. Helgadóttir (2007) describes an experiment she conducted on some Masters of Project Management

(MPM) students in Iceland. The aim was to design a way to increase their moral reasoning and to provide them with a base knowledge of moral theories. Helgadóttir built on the work of Loo (2002) by asking the students to stage vignettes from different perspectives using the four classical ethical theories. The findings of the experiment indicate that teaching project leaders in a very succinct manner to think about the ethics of projects will result in a marked change in the way they view project selection, purpose, risks, stakeholders, goals and outcomes. Jónasson (2008) also described the four classical ethical theories to assess ethical risks in projects and argued that, by viewing the theories in terms of ethical opportunities and risks, ethics in project management can be reduced to asking a series of simple but fundamental questions.

FOUR THEORIES

In order to guide project practitioners in normative ethics we have chosen to introduce what we call the Project Ethics Matrix (PEM). This matrix illustrates the four leading theories in Western intellectual history. The PEM, shown in Figure 1.2, is a simplified diagram, designed for pragmatic purposes, showing the four ethical theories: the two *outcome-oriented ethical theories* are virtue ethics and utility ethics, and the two *process-oriented ethical theories* are duty ethics and rights ethics. By systematically considering these guiding principles, project leaders can become aware of the critical ethical issues at stake and take the appropriate action. The process of ethically evaluating a project is essential when it comes to choosing projects, identifying ethical challenges within projects, and preparing actions to meet these challenges.

This grouping of classical ethics theories is a simplification. However, representing the four components in the context of outcome and process is an attempt to generate a common basis for understanding. The first component (upper left) and first aspect of *outcome-oriented ethics* is virtue ethics, with its focus on how people, especially the individual, choose to live their lives, go about their work and strive to excel. The second component and second aspect of *outcome-oriented ethics* is utilitarianism, where the accumulated collective utility of the many is valued. The third component and first aspect of *process-oriented ethics* is duty, where the decision-making agent is supposed to define specific principles that should dictate what is right and what is wrong. The fourth component and second aspect of *process-oriented ethics* consists of principles based on rights, and where the essential rights of people take precedence. Each of these components will be discussed in detail in the following chapters.

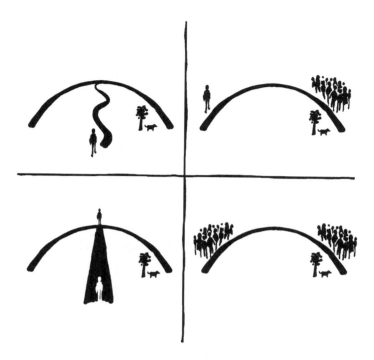

Figure 1.2   The Project Ethics Matrix (PEM) indicating the four main schools of ethical thinking: virtue ethics (upper left), utility ethics (upper right), duty ethics (lower left), rights ethics (lower right)

THE NATURE OF ETHICAL ISSUES

As we have seen above, some interesting work in the field of project management has already dealt directly with the moral aspect of projects. If we go further, however, we see that the ethical dilemmas that one encounters in life ask fundamental questions of us, such as:

- How do the world and the people within it matter to us?
- What do we value and what is essential for our well-being and happiness?
- How do we ensure that the ethical decision is recognised by others?

Projects usually aim at solving problems – something that has not been done needs to be done. It is up to the project leader to lead that and to make things happen. On the way, the project leader is faced with a variety of problems. Some of these problems are purely technical; others have an ethical dimension. What defines an ethical problem, or an ethical issue, over and against technical problems, is that there are competing values at stake. This is illustrated in Figure 1.3, which shows a rainbow-like line or a spectrum of choices between two options. On each end one should imagine a value (wealth, security, friendship, profit, and so on) and on the other a competing value. In many cases the values at stake are not only two but many, but for the sake of clarification the figure symbolises the tension between opposing values.

Figure 1.3   Ethics is finding the balance between competing values

Although food, shelter, security, social recognition and the ability to self-actualise are of importance, they might have decreasing worth if there is a lack of moral capital such as justice, love, friendship, judgement and self-determination in our lives. Moral capital is the overall capacity of an individual, a team, an organisation or a society to be considerate of ethical and social responsibilities and to act sustainably in such that it aims for what is true, right and beautiful. It originates in our interconnection with other beings and it has been demonstrated since time immemorial that moral qualities are, despite their subjective nature, necessary to sustain personal integrity, society, livelihood and even life. This moral capital must be recognised as such and aligned with the values of stakeholders, and congruent with the objectives of the project.

At a personal level, ethics offers us guidance in coping through the life cycles of the project that is our life, taking into consideration our nature, sins, ignorance and inability to judge; and helping us to understand the real value of things. Ethics is also concerned with the link between the more idiosyncratic morality of the individual, that we could call 'myself ethics', and what we could call 'all of us ethics', that has a more collective flavour. For our purpose, one of the fundamental questions that is relevant in this case could be: why should we be moral if it pays better to stay ethically ignorant? We will address that question and other dilemmas in the following chapters.

Case 2 – Bao and RECELD

Bao, who has a BA degree as a social worker and is an IPMA-certified project leader (C level) is a project leader with considerable international experience. She is commissioned to assist in the carrying out of the project 'RECELD', which includes the recruitment and training of new personnel for a large private operator in the elderly care sector. The salaries offered for different positions are negotiable, although the project owner has made it clear to Bao that the bottom line in terms of cost is the most important selection factor, and Bao has been highly incentivised to seek the lowest costs for her client, who is known for excellence in cost efficient operations.

Upon reviewing the terms and conditions of employment, Bao is convinced that mistakes in recruitment could be made in this case to those made several years previously in another place, where a poor recruitment policy had resulted in a widespread scandal because of overemphasis on efficiency in the care of the elderly.

Questions:

- Are there ethical issues involved in this case?
- What could be the ethical issues at stake?
- What could be the competing values in this case?
- Should Bao discuss her ethical considerations with the project owner, and if so, how?
- What can Bao do in this case?

BUSINESS, ENGINEERING AND SELF-ACTUALISATION

Some projects are 'for profit', while others aim for the common good. To discuss in any detail the ethical domains of the former would bring us deep into discourse regarding whether it is the primary role, or even the sole role, of wealth-seeking enterprises to increase the wealth of their owners, or to balance this with fostering the growth and development of all. No matter how we answer this question, those of us affiliated with the field of project management, wanting to view ourselves as free, meaning-seeking, active agents, must dare to think about the context and wider implications of our actions. For business organisations at large, this is a question of strategy. For project leaders and project teams, the questions at stake surface in the more detailed actualisation within the wider organisational strategy and objectives. From an ethical perspective, we could define project management as a variety of methods used to reach certain well-defined goals by deploying technology, personnel and other resources to add, refine or create something new that delivers change, value to the owners and, hopefully, good for the world.

In the business sector and in economic terms, project management hence becomes the *visible hand* working under the providence and supervision of what Adam Smith (1723–1790) called the invisible hand of the markets. This Scottish social philosopher argued that in a free market and with healthy competition, individual profit-seeking endeavours are led collectively by an invisible hand towards the common good, and that this would be so even if every project were aimed primarily at the maximisation of the wealth of the project owner. This was later dubbed the 'laissez-faire theory' of governmental influence upon trade and commercial actualisations. On the other hand, experience has shown that even though the principle of free trade and the law of supply and demand seem to provide essential guidance, when it comes to the efficiency and distribution of wealth, they might not cover all moral domains. It is important, therefore, for all involved in the field of project management also to look for other guiding principles to identify, assess and manage possible ethical risk in projects.

GUIDES, BOOKS OF KNOWLEDGE AND ETHICAL CODES

Ethics features in professional guidelines for project leaders to the extent that it is considered to be one of the competences that one must have. This is evidenced by the fact that most project and programme managers' associations and guilds have codes of ethics and/or professional conduct, such as those published by the APM, PMI and IPMA (see the webpages of these associations). For example, the most recent version of the IPMA Competence Baseline (ICB) addresses ethics in a short sub-section in which it defines three interrelated areas of project management competencies: contextual, technical and behavioural. Ethics, in this case, is considered to be one of the behavioural competencies, but it is only discussed very briefly and there is a lack of clarity in how it is presented.

In the IPMA certification system, ethics is addressed at all certification levels. At the lowest level – Level D, Certified Project Management Associate – a candidate must have 'the required knowledge regarding ethics', which sounds unclear in its tone. Higher certification levels demand that the candidate has demonstrated ethics effectively in project situations of increased complexity – wording that still seems rather ambiguous.

Many professional societies of engineers have had ethical codes and codes of conduct for a long time. The American Institute of Electrical and Electronics Engineers (IEEE), for instance, adopted its code of ethics in 1912. The current code provides instructions that aim at safeguarding engineers and protecting the public. This concise document consists of 10 statements that affiliates of the Institute commit themselves to. Topics covered include avoiding conflict of interest, rejecting bribery, seeking and offering honest criticism of technical work, assisting colleagues in professional development and supporting them in following the code of ethics.[2]

The National Society of Professional Engineers (NSPE) in the United States issued its original code of ethics in 1946. It has been modified since then and the most recent version is comprehensive and addresses such aspects as public safety, technical competence, data accuracy, conflict of interest, professional behaviour and professional development. The International Federation of Consulting Engineers (FIDIC) has also issued a code of ethics. This is a short, concise document addressing such aspects as competence, integrity, impartiality, fairness to others and corruption.

The European Federation of National Engineering Associations (FEANI) acknowledges that the decisions and conduct of engineers can have a major impact on both the environment and society. The engineering profession has, for that reason, an obligation to guarantee that it works in the public interest and with complete respect for health, safety and sustainability. The code of conduct issued by FEANI states that engineers should maintain their competences, not misrepresent their educational qualifications, be capable of providing impartial analysis, carry out their tasks so as to prevent avoidable danger, accept appropriate responsibility for their work, respect people's personal rights and be prepared to contribute to the public debate on matters of technical understanding in fields where they are competent to comment.

The history of ethical consideration within the project management community is shorter; however, awareness has grown in recent years. The British APM has issued a code of professional conduct stating that professionalism and ethics relate to proper, acceptable conduct. The organisation states that 'Ethics covers the conduct and moral principles recognised within the association as appropriate for the project and programme management profession' (APM, 2004). The code of conduct discusses the personal responsibilities of members and such topics as honesty, respect, the duty to act in the best interests of employers and clients, keeping professional skills up to date, and claiming expertise only in appropriate areas. Responsibility to the profession and the association is also addressed. All members must explicitly commit to this code as a condition of membership and a process is in place to hold them accountable to it.

The IPMA addresses ethics in its body of knowledge as part of the IPMA Competence Baseline as discussed above but, at the time of writing of this book,

---

2   www.ieee.org/membership_services/membership/ethics_code.html.

this has yet to be issued in the form of a code of conduct or as specific ethical guidelines.

PROJECT ETHICS IN PRACTICE: ICELANDIC SURVEY

In order to bring the topic to life, we recently commissioned a survey to obtain empirical evidence on the perception of ethics amongst up-to-date IPMA-certified project leaders in Iceland. The outline of this survey is introduced below and a brief summary of some findings is given. The results are also occasionally referred to in later chapters.

The survey, conducted online by Sigurður Fjalar Sigurðarson consisted of a number of closed questions to gauge whether project leaders consider ethical factors as critical success factors in their projects, and to find out if and how they identify and evaluate those factors.

Iceland represents a valid case study in this regard, not only because the authors have easy access to the majority of professional project leaders in the country, but also because management practice within the country has, in recent years, suffered from a lack of ethical decision-making in particular sectors. This is (often) seen as a contributing factor to the major collapse of the Icelandic economy. Despite this, Icelanders seem to be quite capable of organising themselves around catastrophes such as economic meltdowns and volcanic eruptions, and this perceived resilience makes it an interesting international case study in how to react to change and adversity from the project management viewpoint.

A total of 220 IPMA-certified project leaders working in their different fields in Iceland were invited to take part in the survey, and the response rate was 46 per cent; 52 per cent of respondents were female and 48 per cent were male, with an age range from 21 to 60. A breakdown of the different sectors within which the respondents were employed is given in Figure 1.4, from which it can be seen that they were a broadly representative grouping.

The category of 'Other than above mentioned' includes areas such as public research, software development, aircraft leasing, the fishing industry, agriculture, consulting and non-profit projects. The project management experience levels of the survey respondents are shown in Figure 1.5.

The survey revealed that 71–79 per cent of the project leaders normally define success criteria for cost, time and quality aspects of projects, but only 55 per cent define success criteria for customer satisfaction (Sigurðarson, 2009). It also showed that 42–47 per cent of projects are completed on time, on budget, and meet other project specifications, such as quality. Even though not all projects are completed within the predefined boundaries, most are nevertheless regarded as successful and make a positive impression on the customer, project team and organisation.

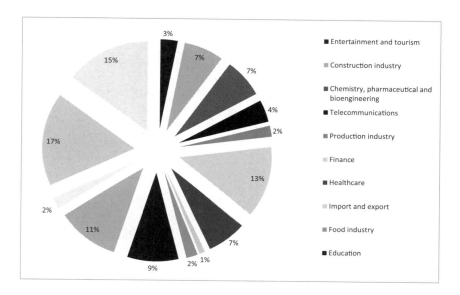

Figure 1.4   Areas of employment for those who answered the Iceland project ethics survey

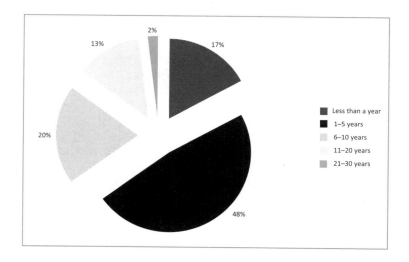

Figure 1.5   Project management experience levels of those surveyed

With regard to ethics, however, fewer than half of the project leaders reported having the proper tools to identify, evaluate and deal with moral issues within projects; and only about one-third claimed to conduct an ethical risk assessment in their projects. The reason these latter do so at all might be because project leaders with a MPM degree from the MPM programme in Iceland have been encouraged during their education to carry out an ethical risk assessment, and IPMA-certified project leaders, in order to qualify for certification, must have at least a basic understanding of what ethics could entail in project management.

The project success statements in the survey were largely based on the 'Project Success Assessment Questionnaire' introduced in the book *Reinventing Project Management* by Shenhar and Dvir (2007). A novel inclusion in our study was a list of questions related to the ethical scope of projects and to what extent moral reflection is seen as an essential part of professional project management. To do this we created a framework based on the four normative ethical theories – virtue ethics, utility ethics, duty ethics and rights ethics – which are used for evaluating ethical considerations among practitioners in their projects on five interrelated levels. To verify the usefulness and comprehensiveness of those statements, we began by trialling them in the classroom in the Master of Project Management.

CONDUCT, DEMEANOUR AND MANAGEMENT

It may not be easy to define succinctly what makes an ethical project leader, but we can, at this stage, list some key attributes:

- They allow and encourage discussion of ethical issues around their projects.
- They are able to identify and tackle ethical concerns pre-emptively or as they arise.
- They have a fundamental understanding of ethical theory and see it as an essential part of the professional managerial tool box.
- They are able to apply ethical reasoning, seeing it as their responsibility to conduct an ethical risk assessment in projects, and have the ability to execute such an assessment.
- They are aware of their responsibilities when it comes to the welfare and safety of the team; they take moral responsibility as a member of a civilised society.
- They are able to communicate the reasons for their ethical decisions to stakeholders.

Below is a summary of how Icelandic project leaders fare in these respects:

- 51 per cent agreed (or strongly agreed) that conversations about ethical issues do take place in their projects; 29 per cent disagreed (or strongly disagreed).
- 54 per cent agreed (or strongly agreed) that ethical issues come up in projects they manage; 22 per cent disagreed (or strongly disagreed).
- 95 per cent agreed (or strongly agreed) that knowledge in ethical theory should be a part of the project leader's skill-set; none disagreed but 5 per cent were neutral.
- 90 per cent agreed (or strongly agreed) that they had studied ethical theory; 6 per cent disagreed (or strongly disagreed).

In our study we asked people to respond to the following statements:

1. Measurable goals in terms of time are always defined in my projects.
2. Measurable goals in terms of cost are always defined in my projects.
3. Measurable goals in terms of quality are always defined in my projects.
4. Measurable goals in terms of customer satisfaction are always defined in my projects.

Seventy-nine per cent of the respondents said that they define measurable time goals for their projects, 70 per cent define measurable cost goals, 71 per cent define measurable quality goals, but only 55 per cent define measurable goals for customer satisfaction. The difference between the customer satisfaction criteria and the other project success criteria is interesting as it indicates either that considerably less emphasis is placed on customer satisfaction than on the other criteria, or that there is considerable difficulty devising ways to measure customer satisfaction.

It can be concluded that these project leaders generally define project success criteria according to the traditional concerns of time, cost and quality, with less emphasis on customer satisfaction, while ethical soundness has not yet gained a solid foothold as a core indicator of project success. However, this might be changing, but only to a limited extent, with the emphasis now shifting more towards sustainability in projects. As in the project management field in general, sustainability seems to search for its justifications solely in the realm of utility. This failure to apply ethical theory in project management is a weakness, given that ethics is all about successful self-actualisation, prosperity and well-being – precisely what should define critical successes and development.

Questions for reflection:

- How do you initiate ethical awareness in your projects?
- How do you present ethics as something that should be part of decision-making?
- How do you facilitate conversation on ethical issues in your projects?
- What kind of ethical issues arise in your projects?
- What do you know about ethical theory?
- Why should ethical theory be part of the skills set of project leaders?
- How is it the project leader's responsibility to conduct an ethical risk assessment in his or her projects?
- How is it the project owner's responsibility to conduct an ethical risk assessment in his or her projects?
- How do you go about doing risk assessment in your projects?
- Why should you do ethical risk assessment in your projects?
- Why should ethical risk assessment be conducted in projects?
- How is the project leader responsible for project finance?
- How is the project leader responsible for the welfare of the project team?
- How can knowledge of ethical theory strengthen the project leader is his or her decision-making?
- How can projects impact negatively on people's rights?
- What tools do you have to evaluate ethical risk in projects?
- When should you bring in a specialist in ethical theory to evaluate your projects?

CHAPTER 2

OUTCOME-ORIENTED ETHICS: VIRTUE ETHICS

If ethics are poor at the top, that behavior is copied down through the organisation.

Robert Noyce, inventor of the silicon chip

> Fully informed and with a clear conscience, are you sure that the project outcome will contribute to the long-term well-being of key agents/stakeholders/interested parties?

VIRTUE ETHICS

Virtue ethics is concerned with the character and motivations of a person, and how they will ensure that decisions taken by individuals during their life will be made in pursuit of the greater good. As such, virtue ethics is less about actual outcomes, but rather how we approach our role in determining those outcomes, with the broader argument being that if one follows the path of virtuous ethics, then positive outcomes are most likely to result. In this sense virtue ethics are outcome ethics.

Virtue ethics has a long documented history dating back at least to the early Greek philosophers and is to be found in varying guises in all the world's major religions. It is most often summarised as a list of individual virtues or desirable character traits that may also include short explanations as to how they are to be interpreted. For example, below is a list of virtues drawn up by the soon-to-be-famous American Benjamin Franklin to guide him in his future endeavours. As a young adult (aged 20 in 1726), he was perceived by himself and some others at that stage in his life as a failure:

1. Temperance: Eat not to dullness; drink not to elation.
2. Silence: Speak not but what may benefit others or yourself; avoid trifling conversation.
3. Order: Let all your things have their places; let each part of your business have its time.

4. Resolution: Resolve to perform what you ought; perform without fail what you resolve.
5. Frugality: Make no expense but to do good to others or yourself; that is, waste nothing.
6. Industry: Lose no time; be always employed in something useful; cut off all unnecessary actions.
7. Sincerity: Use no hurtful deceit; think innocently and justly; speak accordingly.
8. Justice: Wrong none by doing injuries; or omitting the benefits of your duty.
9. Moderation: Avoid extremes; forbear resenting injuries so much as you think they deserve.
10. Cleanliness: Tolerate no uncleanliness in body, clothes, or habitation.
11. Tranquility: Be not disturbed at trifles or at accidents common or unavoidable.
12. Chastity: Rarely use venery but for health or offspring, never to dullness, weakness, or the injury of your own or another's peace or reputation.
13. Humility: Emulate Christ and Socrates in all things.

Throughout the remainder of the eighteenth century, until his death in 1790, Franklin used these virtues as guides, going on to become one of the most productive, successful and self-actualised people of his time. Some of his many achievements include setting up a library, a hospital, an insurance company, a fire company, being responsible for a broad range of scientific observations and inventions such as the lightning rod, being the first American Ambassador to France, and helping to write the Declaration of Independence and the American Constitution. In his memoirs, written shortly before his death, Franklin acknowledged the importance of these virtues in his achievements, although he was not so sure he had upheld the thirteenth virtue of humility, which had actually been suggested to him as an addition after a Quaker friend of his had reviewed his original 12 virtues!

It is undoubtedly the case that Franklin was a great project leader to have achieved these goals within his lifetime. It is indeed a useful exercise for the modern professional project leader to reflect on his approach and how it compares to his or her own value system. This is only one example of a person who has tried to live according to virtue, however, and an inherent point of contention in the debate on the importance of virtue ethics on professional behaviour has been the subjective nature of what are considered to be desirable virtues.

THE ORIGIN OF VIRTUE ETHICS

Ever since antiquity, theorists have been interested in defining virtue and in what makes a person good in what he or she is supposed to be good at. The question of what it takes to be a good professional in the broadest sense has, therefore, always been present, even though we might now be faced with an increased sense of urgency owing to our capacity for being a serious impact on our human and natural environment. The Greek philosophers Socrates, Plato and Aristotle all advocated virtue ethics, and virtue ethics were for a long time the predominant ethics in Europe. Aristotle is probably the most famous of the group. His classic *Nicomachean Ethics* embodies his approach to ethics and went on to become a highly influential work and the core of medieval philosophy.

Aristotle showed his analytical skills and determination in his intellectual project that aimed to explain the nature of all things in a unified system. He was not just an outstanding thinker but also a practical man with strong managerial skills which he used to define, plan and implement his main project – to establish his own school, Lyceum, in Athens in 355 BCE. He explained virtue in very simple terms and almost as a mathematical measure. This approach suits the way engineering-inclined project leaders assess problems and search for solutions – the knowledge that ethics is able to use quantifiable measures in decision-making comes in handy.

Virtue for Aristotle was the mean or balance between too much and too little of certain character traits. For example, courage is the balance between cowardice and stupidity, abundance is the balance between scarcity and excess, and generosity is the balance between tightness and profligacy. He defined virtue, therefore, as the golden mean or the golden path between two extremes, which we can illustrate in Figure 2.1.

Aristotle's approach to ethics was teleological – denoting the study of meaning or purpose – and virtue is what defines excellence in the quality of something and serves well its purpose. He was one of the first great philosophers to really focus on the study of ethics and, to him, ethics was much more than just a moral, religious or legal concept. He considered ethics to be a practical study that aimed at doing good, rather than building up knowledge for its own sake. This practical wisdom can also be referred to as prudence. Virtue for Aristotle has to do with the

Figure 2.1   Virtue is the golden mean, or the golden path, between two extremes

proper function (*ergon*) of a thing. An ear is only a good ear insomuch as it can hear, because hearing is the proper function of an ear. A knife is only a good knife if it is sharp. Therefore, a virtuous knife is an excellent knife that is exceptionally sharp. Applied to our topic, we could ask:

- What does a good-quality project leader do?
- What is a good project?

Aristotle reasoned that humans must have a function specific to humans, and that this function must be an activity of the human mind. In his view, the highest good is related to the concept he called *eudemonia*, which denotes well-being or flourishing in the broader sense, rather than an individual feeling of contentment or pleasure.

If one were to embrace the concept of *eudemonia*, then one would believe that there is an important role for us in the greater scheme of things, where meaningful evolution is a purpose that is unique to us humans. The argument goes as follows: the meaning of our function in the world cannot consist only of growth and nourishment, because this we share with plants; nor can it be just be based on the life of the senses, for this we share with animals; so this unique human function must have to do with our peculiarly human faculty of reason. The highest human good is, therefore, an excellence in human functioning, enabled by the good exercise of reason. This must, necessarily, and maybe especially, hold for good project leaders and project teams who, by definition, strive for excellence in their work professionally.

In order to achieve this state, Aristotle espoused the concept of virtue and went on to explain that achieving a virtuous character requires the good fortune to receive the appropriate education and experience. This, he argued, leads to a later stage in which one consciously chooses to do the best thing, and to train oneself to approach life in this way will gradually develop into practical wisdom. Thus, virtue lies on the middle path of the golden means. To follow it does not take a lot of expertise, but rather an honest deliberation and use of common sense; it is the critical path that leads both to personal happiness and professional integrity.

PRACTICAL WISDOM

Defining professional virtues, however, might not be all that easy for the modern project leader, as the field is wide and professional paths are very varied. The project leader is faced with different managerial responsibilities, such as calculations, risk management, human resource management, negotiation and controlling. Also, the times are changing; the terrain is not getting smaller, but rather much bigger and much broader. In all probability, however, Aristotle would have said that only project leaders who aim for the highest good are good project leaders, and only *they* could be said to be competent and truly good advocates of their profession. He would also, most likely, have claimed that the only projects worth pursuing are those that are planned and intended for the sake of the highest good.

If one tries to define the highest good, probably the first idea would be to define it in terms of pleasure. These pleasures could be the *sensual pleasures* of food and drink, sex, or those which are often linked with project management, namely the pleasures of monetary gain and riches. There might also be *aesthetic pleasures* and *intellectual pleasures* such as the longing to excel in project management; or they might be *political pleasures* acquired by virtuous political action, or the pleasures of scientific research or philosophical contemplation. From the Aristotelian perspective, though, all of these definitions are too narrow. What they lack is a determination to participate in the betterment of society as a whole. In order to achieve such an outcome, it is, in Aristotle's view, necessary to be guided by a strong sense of virtue ethics.

In describing virtue ethics, Aristotle defined two types of virtues: moral virtues and intellectual virtues. Moral virtues are exemplified by courage, temperance and liberty, while the key intellectual virtues are exemplified by wisdom and understanding. Moral virtues are the *practical wisdom* that is gradually acquired by courage, temperance and liberty of choice in *real situations*. For the project leader this is the capability to consider the mode of action in order to solve problems for the client and to deliver change – and, more precisely, in line with Aristotle, a change that enhances the quality of life.

Quality of life relates to concepts such as a standard of living, freedom, human rights and happiness and the ability to realise one's potential. Even though Aristotle defined happiness as the highest good, in modern times, where economics dominates, happiness is deemed subjective and hard to measure. Other abstract measures, often denoted as income, percentages or indices, gain priority. However, happiness clearly does not necessarily increase in line with the comfort that results from growing income; there are obviously many other contributory factors including, very importantly, a strong sense of fulfilment – namely that we achieve the goals which we set ourselves in life and make use of our inherent talents. In obtaining this, we require practical wisdom to decide how to achieve a certain outcome and the ability to reflect upon and determine that outcome.

Practical wisdom does not come automatically or solely from theoretical speculation. Just like all real project-leader knowledge, it is only built up through a maturation process where it is practised and tried out. We need, therefore, to be taught and trained in it to accomplish it. Practical wisdom is naturally concerned with both universal truths and the particular situations to which they can be applied to. Because of this, it can only become known and understood from experience.

We can learn the principles of action, but applying them in the real world, in delicate or unforeseen situations, requires experience of the world. For example, in business and professional consulting, information can be of utmost importance, particularly in the areas of intellectual property and client confidentiality, and one needs to maintain a careful balance between honesty and discretion.

Case 3 – Abdul-Hakim and Creatag

Abdul-Hakim is a PMP-certified project leader and a recently appointed project leader in the creative department of an international advertising agency called Creatag, with a large project portfolio. Abdul-Hakim begins to suspect that two junior employees with rising-star reputations are taking ideas from another junior employee, who is very talented but introverted, and passing them off as their own completed work. During the time of Abdul-Hakim's predecessor, it is quite likely that this situation had already been occurring, but the department as a whole had done extremely well financially out of it. The junior employees with the star reputations also have close links with people higher up in the company and are very successful in their eyes in increasing customer sales.

Questions:

- What are the competing values?
- What are the ethical issues at stake?
- How should Abdul-Hakim prepare himself to confront the issue?
- How should he address this case?

WHAT TO DO?

Project management will be defined here more in terms of practical wisdom rather than theoretical wisdom, although it should, of course, take notice of scientific exploration and theoretical speculations. Finally, however, project management is about dealing with the dynamic reality of human attitudes, group dynamics, uncertainties, and the serious fact that it is possible for one unpredictable human being to cause a lot of damage. It lies at the very heart of project management that we should ask the following questions and rely on our practical wisdom for the answers (Flyvbjerg, 2001).

- Where are we going?
- Where should we be going?
- Who will gain?

- Who will suffer?
- Is this development desirable?
- What should we do about it?

If we now try to create a practical tool that project leaders can use to define virtue in their decision-making processes, we could say:

- Make sure that the results of your projects will truly show/reveal your virtuous use of reason for the sake of the highest good.
- Only choose projects that you are capable of carrying out for the sake of the highest good.
- Execute your projects in such a way that their outcomes always show/reveal respect for the human function of bringing about the highest good.

BEING GOOD AT WHAT WE DO

Let us now assume that it is an integral part of being a professional project leader to be good at what we do – namely to define, plan and execute projects. Even though such a definition helps, we might want to define in much greater detail what this means. Does being a good project leader mean to follow prescribed standards and procedures? Or, can we look at it from a more close-up and personal perspective, allowing each of us to define for ourselves – as professionals – what our professional 'goodness' should entail?

The typical approach to defining professionalism is in terms of *professional competences*. At the job interview stage, this may be a list of desired attributes that are included in the job description; in a mid-career review it may take the form of a number of headings under which people are assessed. Increasingly, it appears that competence is being measured quantitatively as opposed to qualitatively, and metrics are finding their way into all walks of life. In academia, for example, the numbers of papers or articles published and the numbers of related citations are often used to assess people, with little regard as to whether these works were truly groundbreaking, or whether the citations were positive or negative. In this situation the chances that a star performer who does not have a solid background to fall back on will be exposed for his or her lack of knowledge or wisdom further down the line can be high; meanwhile, they may have caused damage to their employer. In the long run, quality can matter, particularly within professions with a long history of regard for excellence reflected in their ethical codes.

As a project leader, you may feel that your future career progression is best aided by being seen to have faithfully followed other people's leads in a prescribed fashion. Undoubtedly, many successful careers have been built on such pragmatism, and the avoidance of conflict or controversy. There is, however, the danger in this case that not being honest with oneself or others during the course of a project in the broader sense can mean poor decision-making goes unchecked. This may increase the risk of a negative event which can damage the outcome and one's reputation.

There is both agreement and disagreement in these matters in the modern literature, with one good example being the review by Gilbert Harman of Princeton University of the 1999 book *On Virtue Ethics* by Rosalind Hursthouse (Harman, 1999). Both of these authors are respected in the field of ethics. Hursthouse is often described as a neo-Aristotelian, while Harman is known to prefer a form of moral relativism. What is apparent from this and other exchanges between eminent ethicists is how finely nuanced ethical decisions can become, and what tends to work in normal practice can be questionable in particular circumstances. This is often conveyed using abstract theoretical reasoning. However, if you are a programme manager in a hospital with the responsibility to implement severe budget cuts as part of an austerity drive, then you are faced with the stark reality of deciding what the least bad options are, and there will always be certain groups that suffer as a result.

Another example may be where you are given the task of setting up a regional product manufacturing line in a particular area where prior political negotiation has stipulated that local employment be provided whenever possible. This starting position can be challenged if it becomes apparent that the skill levels and quality control of the local workforce are not sufficient, and you, as a project leader, have to work out solutions to these problems. In this case one could decide on a number of different options, including accepting these lower standards in order to maintain stability, bringing in skilled workers from elsewhere regardless of the political consequences, taking it upon oneself to motivate and train the current workforce, or a mixture of these approaches. In this case, the different groups, such as senior management, local workforce, other local stakeholders, or neutral commentators will judge the decisions that you make in different ways. Being a good project leader in this case means achieving the most broadly satisfactory outcome without compromising on quality, and being able to communicate this to stakeholders.

This last point is important as one could conceivably think of a situation where a project leader, particularly if he is local to the area himself, may become overly close to the other local employees and, in doing so, chooses to ignore cases of poor practice. When consequently a negative incident occurs it could be so serious as to lead to a decision by external senior management to close the facilities, or at the least to cut back on future investment there, which would be a bad outcome for all concerned. In this example, virtue ethics should guide us as project leaders to maintain a certain distance in our dealings with other employees so that we are capable of making the necessary decisions to maintain the greater good, however that may be achieved.

As a project manager, being good at what you do means not only foreseeing and pre-empting problems that are likely to occur, but also having the capacity to competently deal with changing or unexpected circumstances. Virtue ethics provides a solid foundation for achieving this outcome as it prepares one to think about the full consequences of one's decisions, being in the right frame of mind to execute those decisions, and being able to live with those decisions once they are made.

THE COMPETENT PROJECT LEADER

We see from the above that there is a strong personal component in virtue theory. It is ultimately the individuals within the team, organisation or society, who have to define for themselves their notion of virtue. In defining our virtues we may draw on the experience of others, whether writers on the subject, or family, friends, co-workers, superiors and/or professional guilds. It is ultimately up to us, however, to define our virtues in the form of values or ideals that we deem as the right ones to follow and on which we will not want to compromise.

This is both the strength and the weakness of the theory. It is its strength, as it demands self-determination, self-reflection and commitment towards self, rather than delegating the decision-making authority to someone else. It is, therefore, rather existential in nature as it states that our actions will define who we are and nothing else. It is a weakness as it could lead to relativisms, such as the case of the project leader who sees obedience to ill-intentioned authority as his or her core value. Another example could be project leaders who believe that they are above others in society and define their values accordingly. Again, this would probably be based on a lack of deliberation as it fails to take into consideration the need for mutuality and wider consequences in its argumentation.

The divisions between one's private life, on the one hand, and one's professional life, on the other, can often become blurred. While the private life of an individual is not the focus of this book, it could be argued that a project leader who is not able to manage his own private life might also struggle with his professional life, as the two are inevitably intertwined. In light of this, what constitutes the competences of the successful professional project leader?

Our belief is that a competent project leader has to be a talented person who is able to motivate himself, is able to foresee the broad development of the project and the likely pitfalls, who has learnt an essential set of skills in terms of understandings – for example, common sense values and social skills – and who is decisive when necessary. In order to be able to fulfil their role, they have to be able to assess and take into account the interests of the different stakeholders in the project environment: clients, institutions, contractors and specialists, local community;

and they need to be able to make good decisions that are beneficial to and are appropriate for the project. These decisions should not only take into consideration the clients and the most immediate parties that surround the project, but also what affect they will have on the well-being of the individual project leaders themselves, the well-being of the team, the organisation, broader society, the impact on the natural environment, and so on.

Case 4 – Marisol and Chemouflage

Marisol, an IPMA-certified senior project leader (B level), is the project leader of a research division in a big chemical company. She is coming to the final phase of a large project, and is being pressured by senior management to make a presentation to a number of potential investors in a few days on the results to date and future investment opportunities in a major research project with the working title 'Chemouflage'. They know that the sales people in the company have already made a number of claims relating to the new product they are developing, but Marisol and her project team feel that a few key claims are unsubstantiated by the current evidence. The reason they suspect this to be the case is that their own spot checks on the results of the research team have identified discrepancies which are difficult to explain in the short time available. Although they are not 100 per cent certain, they have only recently come to believe that this is due to a lack of rigour on the part of some researchers in the group and that key decisions taken during the testing phase of the project may have been based on flawed information.

Questions:

- What are the ethical issues involved in this case?
- What are the competing values?
- How does this relate to virtue?
- What could Marisol do?

Project management associations globally approach the challenge of defining competent project leaders by designing their certification process such that certified individuals will have the requisite level of knowledge and experience to fulfil their project management roles. This development is part of a steady trend towards turning project management into a profession. With this comes the need to define in more specific terms what is required to fulfil the role of a professional. If project management is turning into a profession then we need to ask: what attributes define a good professional in the profession of project management?

Different project management associations have answered this question in similar but yet somewhat different ways. For example, the International Project Management Association (IPMA) has described project management in terms of three main competence areas that the professional project leader is required to know. These are: (1) technical competences, (2) contextual competences and (3) behavioural competences.

Technical competences relate to the traditional project management disciplines of cost, time and quality management and the mastery of a set of technical methods that incorporate these criteria and are used to prepare and execute projects. Contextual competences relate to the context of the project, its connection with its environment, and the link between the project and the parent organisation through sponsorship, procedures, portfolio and programmes. Behavioural competences relate to the way people react to the challenges of leadership, conflict, communication and personal development.

The Project Management Institute (PMI) has defined project management competences in terms of nine knowledge areas: management of cost, time, scope, quality, human resources, risk, communication, procurement and integration. The areas in this approach are somewhat different from the IPMA, which gives more attention to aspects of human behaviour, relationships and communication. In our view, an important aspect that is missing in the above lists of competences is something that relates more directly to the motivations and personality of the project leader and their sense of values.

COMPETENCE AND COMMITMENT

If we take the idea of the professional role model further, we could say that the idea of a professional calling has both 'personal' and 'universal' implications. This would encompass our role in making our own contribution to civilisation in the broader sense and, therefore, not only being willing to work for one's own good but also for the good of society at large. It could entail rising above narrow forms of egoism, tribalism and nationalism, and involve a dedication to excellence and the willingness to bear responsibility for helping 'spread the possibilities for all people by shaping a genuine cosmopolitan civilisation' (Stackhouse, 1995). In a pluralistic society there are many professions that strive to install these fundamental characteristics of a civilisation. In this sense, we can say that the professional is called upon not only to accept, but also to reform or change the world for the better in a responsible way. The newly emerging field of sustainable management is based on this outlook and the recognition that problems exist where limited resources are pitted against our limitless desires.

This sense of idealism, however, often collides with the realities of project management, where we are dealing with negative factors such as scarcity, conflicting interests, corruption, mistakes, competing perspectives, and group dynamics. Therefore, the idea that we could rid ourselves of uncertainty and human limitations is an illusion. Projects managers inevitably have to deal with the complex imperfect realities that are their self, team, organisation and society, and it takes a strong commitment to retain one's sense of direction and determination in the course of carrying out one's role.

The former president of Iceland, Vigdís Finnbogadóttir, when asked about virtue in the context of engineering ethics, claimed that virtue is essential to strengthen both personal and professional self-image. The virtues she learnt as a young girl were wisdom, temperance, faith, hope, love and friendliness and these remained her guides throughout her later professional life. Virtue, in general, and professional virtue, in particular, are about self-respect and not treating others in ways that we would not want to be treated ourselves. For the aspiring project leader, this means that one should embrace critical thinking and have an interest in self-reflection, meaning, culture and philosophy. This is something that Aristotle would have emphasised when he introduced the golden mean between the two extremes. In times of strategic actions and competitive aggression it is good to remember that Aristotle criticised the Spartans for training their men for war instead of for peace. In a similar vein, he might criticise modern society's failure to train our project leaders towards sustainability and compassion.

PROFESSIONALISM

Professionals provide advice and services in exchange for remuneration, and their knowledge comes from their education, training and their ability to apply it. They are most often members of a professional guild or association and would traditionally have obtained a recognised qualification in a specialised field. While more positions may have been available in the past for those with standard degrees, the increasing level of specialisation and competition within certain sectors in recent times has meant that master degrees and higher are now often a prerequisite for professional recognition. Professionals are expected to have an extensive understanding of their particular profession, the key aspect being that they are trusted on the basis of their professional competence and knowledge. Most professionals are thus held up to strict ethical and moral regulations that their chosen profession collectively defines for itself.

Given the previous discussion, we can now conclude that being a professional is not just a career path; it is a combination of education and training, and includes a moral sense and a sense of motivation. A professional has a positive attitude towards the profession, is loyal towards clients and highly aware of his or her duty towards them. People who enter the old professions such as architecture, engineering and public administration are expected to be competent and to live more or less decent personal lives, or at least lives that do not undermine their work and professional abilities in any way. They are expected to make decisions on morally justifiable grounds, protect the interests of the shareholders they serve, and be aware of what is at stake for the stakeholders. They are also expected to contribute to theory and practice, respect their colleagues and use their skills to enhance the quality of life in society. It is, therefore, expected that professionals not only serve their own needs, but also the needs of society. This standpoint can be challenged, however, by some who would deny any wider responsibility for the general order of things and would reduce their profession 'just to business', where utility, short-term profitability, and the building of wealth for shareholders is the name of the game (Stackhouse, 1995).

In our many discussions with project leaders from different sectors with experience of working all over the world, we have frequently heard the sentiment: 'When I found the field of project management, I felt at home.' This type of response can be considered part of a process of discovery. Professionals provide advice and services in exchange for remuneration; and their knowledge comes from their education and training. Project management as a discipline is relatively new and just like many of the other managerial professions it might not yet be deemed as a profession in the same sense as the old established professions of engineering, medicine, and the church. It is still in the maturation process of becoming a profession in the truest sense and is still widely perceived as a career path, much like many other managerial fields.

While some project leaders might view their professionalism as requiring them to look beyond their immediate responsibilities, seeing themselves acting in the context of the greater good, others consider this viewpoint as very foreign, to say the least. The general trend, it seems, as can be seen in the variety of competence manuals for project leaders, is to view the project leader in the context of vocational training – a person who has dedicated him or herself to meet the needs of a project owner and who is committed to trustworthy standards. The focus is most often on the idea of serving another agent – a client or someone higher up the decision chain. In this sense, to be professional is to do an excellent job even though it has nothing to do with moral duties or the greater order of things. Based on this interpretation, it might be more accurate to speak of a career than a calling, where a career can be defined as a 'sequence of jobs with increased levels of skills, responsibility, and reward as charted by an organisation'. Such ladders of occupational progress are both necessary to complex economic institutions and can be sources of great opportunity for those who find their way onto the lower rungs. Yet career patterns may be designed or pursued with no sense of wider vision for either souls or civilisation; the negative aspects of many people acting in such a manner may be stored up over time to cause widespread problems at a later date.

In hindsight, it is now clear that a strong culture of self-interest and disregard for long-term consequences were allowed to grow in the banking world in the years leading up to the economic crash in 2007/2008. In Iceland, the high pay offered by the banking industry drew talent away from other sectors and many bright minds were employed in what can only be described as flawed projects, where risks were trivialised and short-term considerations were the only concern. The results of this are now evident in 2012; and it will take a long time to fully recover from the poor decisions that were taken.

It seems, in this case, that many of the hard lessons that had been learnt about prudent banking from events such as the Great Depression which began with the crash of the markets in 1929, had been forgotten. The really dedicated banking professionals, who had an inner sense of virtue and followed a recognised code of ethics, were side-lined in the gold-rush years – with predictable consequences.

COMPLYING WITH VIRTUE

We have noticed on occasion that for project managing engineers in particular, there seems to be a certain stigma attached to ethics and ethical reflections as such. The possible reasons for this are: (1) engineers are trained to do particular things in particular ways – in terms of technological solutions – and might therefore be somewhat sceptical if these ingrained procedures are challenged; (2) engineers are trained to solve problems by simplifying the world they are dealing with, whereas ethical questioning is perceived to have the tendency to make things complicated, messy and difficult to deal with, in its quest for taking into consideration all that is at stake; (3) some engineers are at the front line of global institutional and commercial interests and feel that their conscience is being challenged; and (4) engineers are proud of their profession and do not necessarily see the need to have someone from the 'soft' side of the humanities trying to influence their work.

We have often heard from professionals who deal with the intricacies of human undertakings – engineers, medical doctors and experts in the commercial world – that the problem with ethical experts is that they do not understand the issues at stake, or at least not in sufficient depth. It is true that many ethicists are 'armchair' speculators, with backgrounds in philosophical or theological reflection, who might not always be well-attuned to the managerial practicalities of engineering and project management. Their remarks on such practicalities therefore appear to be arrogant or dismissive statements far removed from the realities of decisions about ordering, or not ordering, bulldozers to rip up a tract of land.

Task-oriented project leaders might rhetorically ask: 'Who has time for this?' And their answer might be: 'Just give us the tools so we can then make our decisions and move from speculation into action.' Technical experts often find the humanistic thinker too wordy, their assumptions either too complicated (say for instance ideas about metaphysical assumptions, or critical theory) or overly simplistic owing to a lack of understanding of technical issues or scientific knowledge. There is a perception that ethics is all about prolonged dialogue and endless coming-together meetings for discussion. Such efforts often seem to come across as time-wasting and lacking the pragmatic force that project management needs to accomplish whatever has been deemed as needed to be accomplished.

The antonym of virtue is vice, and we cannot, therefore, discuss virtue without mentioning some of the most famous vices, namely Gregory 1st seven deadly sins. These are vanity, greed, lust, anger, gluttony, envy and sloth. The first, vanity (or pride), entails self-preoccupation for one's own well-being at the expense of the well-being of others. The second is greed (or avarice or covetousness), which is the desire to possess more than one needs or can use, such as the excessive desire for money and power. The third is lust, which is the excessive sexual desire that detracts from true love. The fourth is anger (or wrath), which entails hate, revenge or denial, and punitive desires that are not just. The fifth is gluttony, an excessive love of pleasure and the overindulgence in food, drink or intoxicants, or a misplaced desire for food as a pleasure for its sensuality. The sixth is envy (or jealousy), which appears in the resentment of others for their possessions and abilities. The seventh is sloth (or laziness), which refers to idleness and the wasting of time and/or other allotted resources so others will have to work harder for useful work to be done.

Reading through the above list, it is apparent when the discussion is framed in this way, namely from the opposite of virtue, that, most often, project leaders who are unable to control their vices will not be good at what they do. This would be particularly the case in larger, more complex projects, where one has to deal with a wide variety of people and has considerable responsibility placed on one's shoulders. The important issue, therefore, is to bring these issues alive and be practical in their proactive management.

Yrsa Sigurðardóttir, engineer and internationally recognised crime writer, was the lead project leader on the GBP 850 million Karahnjukar dam project in Iceland. She tackled the question of the virtuous project leader (at a conference organised by the University of Iceland and the Icelandic Engineering Association) by asking: what, then, are the virtues that should define a professional project leader? Are they different from the virtues of common people? She replied: 'Probably not. There are not so many fundamental human virtues. Project management as a practice, however, pushes them all to the core. The work of a project leader will inevitably bring all of the most important virtues into play. Projects can have many stakeholders and can have a major impact on the environment and society. Project leaders also deal with large amounts of money, cultural diversity, competitive environment, rapid technological development and the need to set standards and educate younger and less experienced practitioners.' (translated from Icelandic)

The most important professional virtues of competent project leaders are, according to Sigurðardóttir, honesty, integrity, compassion and courage. She said: 'Honesty in project estimates and in cooperation entails, for instance, not telling stakeholders just what they want to hear, but the truth about the matter stated in clear ways.' Honesty is essential in many other aspects including how we assess our own work and the work of others, and in our general business dealings. Integrity is essential in all management practice, but especially in control management, conflict resolution and dealing with crises effectively while retaining the support of people. Compassion or empathy enables project leaders to see things from other people's perspective and to be able to work and communicate with a broad spectrum of people on an equal basis and in a way that aims to bring out the best in situations. Most of us have a strong tendency to believe we know things better even though this might not be the case. This might, at first, be difficult to acknowledge but with practice it gets easier and easier, and also more and more rewarding. Courage enables us to pay attention to criticism and state our views clearly. Project leaders should give good advice and we are more professional if we are prepared to speak our mind. Courage is not just a heroic act, but a means to deal with ever-changing times, situations and project environments. There is comfort in dealing with the known and it takes courage to deal with the unknown.

Modern society is complex and a skilful project leader must take a variety of aspects into consideration. He or she works in an environment where there may be a variety of interested parties; where he or she is the leader of teams and so must maintain equilibrium between different individuals; and where he or she must think about nature in a responsible way, keeping sustainability in mind. Project leaders may also be making decisions involving large sums of other people's money, which can place a huge responsibility on them to ensure that the right things are done in the right way. He or she also deals with different cultural environments, and must be able to communicate and develop skills and training in times of fast-paced development.

To conclude, virtue ethics is outcome-oriented and ultimately focuses on our sense of self, as it will be experienced after our project is finished. From the Aristotelian viewpoint, the accumulation of happiness is fully accomplished and can only be seen after the project has been completed and its wider effects become apparent. The virtuous do not want to feel foolish, dishonest, or immoral after the execution of a project; they want to enjoy personal satisfaction from its completion. As we are focused on striving for success and excellence, it is interesting to mention a concept that is directly derived from the notion of virtue, namely the concept of *virtuoso*, meaning prodigy, expert, genius, or a maestro of performance. Is this not what the skilful project leader should be aiming to be? We think so, and Aristotle would probably have thought so too!

In our survey, we tried to capture the project leaders' understanding of virtue. In it 92 per cent agreed with the statement that successful projects are projects that one can be satisfied with when finished, 90 per cent said that they could with pride tell their relatives about their projects, their outcomes and their consequences, and 68 per cent disagreed with the statement that a virtuous project leader is one who does what he is told, while only 8 per cent agreed with this statement.

Questions for reflection:

- On the personal level, what is a truly successful project for you?
- What have been the good personal consequences of your projects?
- What have been the bad personal consequences of your projects?
- What are you proud of in your project management endeavours?
- What are you not proud of in your project management endeavours?
- How do virtue and compliance with duty interfere with your project management?

CHAPTER 3

OUTCOME-ORIENTED ETHICS: UTILITY ETHICS

A business that makes nothing but money is a poor kind of business.
Henry Ford 1863–1947, American industrialist

> Fully informed and with a clear conscience, are you sure that the project outcome will contribute to the long-term collective (accumulated) well-being (more satisfaction/less pain) of the many, including, but not limited to, key agents/stakeholders/interested parties?

UTILITY ETHICS

Virtue has traditionally been the ethical norm of the prudent – and often religiously devoted – project leader, in the ancient world, through the Middle Ages, and all the way up to the dawn of economics as a specialised field in the 18th century. Nowadays, however, while there are still many managers who conduct themselves primarily according to virtue, the idea of utility seems to be becoming more and more the ethical norm. And, what is more, utilitarian ideas and concepts seem to underlie the thinking of Western civilisation both in regard to individual choice and as a paradigm for understanding collective aspiration and behaviour. From this viewpoint, the aim of all projects is utilisation in some form; utilisation should bring utility to the clients and project owner. Utility ethics, however, takes this further in its demand that the outcome of any action to contribute to the collective utility – or in other words, the well-being or happiness – of the many. This is illustrated in Figure 3.1.

The term *utility* is used in an attempt to measure relative satisfaction of any kind of consumption or experience. So an increase in measurable utility is seen as a positive indicator in modern day economic thinking and something to be aspired to. To illustrate this in our survey of Icelandic project leaders, we asked for a response to the following statement: 'successful projects are projects that create more prosperity for many individuals rather than for just a few.' The responses showed neither strong disagreement, nor disagreement; 21 per cent were neutral, 38 per cent agreed, and 41 per cent strongly agreed; 1 per cent thought the question did not apply.

Figure 3.1   Utility ethics aims at maximising utility for as many as possible

To the modern mind, utility is usually associated with increased consumption of goods and services, greater wealth and more leisure. But is this so? In our survey, we asked the participants to respond to the statement 'All my projects aim to increase satisfaction and pleasure': 4 per cent strongly disagreed, 17 per cent disagreed, 35 per cent were neutral, 26 per cent agreed, and 14 per cent strongly agreed; 4 per cent said that the question did not apply.

We see from this that one of the challenges of thinking in terms of utility is the problem of quantifying it. Utility is often defined in terms of an indifference curve that describes the combination of commodities that an agent, be it a project leader, a project team, a project organisation or a society, would accept to maintain a given level of satisfaction. Based on that notion, it is assumed that both individual and social utility can be construed as the dependent variable of a utility function and a social welfare function respectively. When coupled with constraints such as time, cost and quality, these functions can represent what has been named Pareto efficiency, and such a utility analysis plays a major role in most welfare economics.

Nevertheless, utility is difficult to measure directly. As a result, attempts have been made to find methods to measure customer satisfaction or market behaviour assuming that, in a competitive equilibrium, such things might reveal the utility gained by the people involved. These supposed manifestations in price are what the American economist Paul Samuelsson named *revealed preferences*. The economist Alfred Marshall (1842–1924) said that utility correlates to desire or want, and this can only be measured indirectly by what it outwardly indicates, such as in the price of the goods or the price we are willing to pay for the satisfaction of this desire (Marshall, 1920: 78).

Economics distinguishes between two types of utility. One is *cardinal utility*, where the quantity of utility differs in terms of more or less suffering and pleasure, and this can be used as a behavioural or ethical quantity. The other is *ordinal utility*, which just defines a position within the utility function and not the weakness or strength of any utility preferences. Utility functions of both sorts can be used to rank a choice. For example, we can have three projects: Project A has a utility of 1.5 million utils; Project B has a utility of 1.0 million utils; and Project C has a utility of 500,000 utils. When measured in cardinal utility, we could conclude that Project A is better than Project B and, in the same way, Project B is better than Project C.

There is, however, no clear way to interpret how different people value their needs and hence utility. In ordinal utility differences in utils are not of ethical consideration; the utility index would only encode a behavioural ordering between members of a choice set, but tells nothing about the related strength of preferences. In the above example, it would only be possible to say that Project A is preferred to Project B, and Project B to Project C, but no more.

For project choice, the question arises whether you should use cardinal utility as an indicator in analysis, rather than considering agent preferences over choice sets. However, preference relations can often be represented by utility functions satisfying several properties.

Customer satisfaction is one of the main success criteria that traditional project leaders use when designing a project, and the client's preference within a utility function is measured. To do this, project leaders try to define the consumption set of their client, meaning all the mutually exclusive wishes which the client might have; then they will model the choice in a way that is presumably rational and often one-dimensional, quasi-concave, continuous and globally non-satiated.

But could the client, or other stakeholders, have preferences that are not represented by a utility function? We might argue that utility functions should inevitably include all preferences, and, therefore, all preferences concerned with ethical considerations, such as virtue, sense of duty and the rights of others – topics that are explored in other chapters of this book. It could also go the other way and include apathetic, amoral and even outright evil preferences. We can claim that ethical considerations can, either voluntarily or involuntarily, be all too easily dismissed in the name of rational choice and utility. This can be the blind-spot of the rational decision-making tool of utility functions.

Expected utility analysis looks at choices in terms of risks that can have possible multidimensional outcomes. Some definitions of utility make it possible to rank utilities, but not to add them together. Let's take an example. Project X may be more feasible than Project Y, but we might not be able to say that Project X is 100 times more feasible than Project Y. Utility cannot be quantified in this way because of the law of diminishing returns, which states that the utility gained by the first unit of consumption is high, the utility of the next unit is a little less, and all the way up to the point where the utility function of one more unit consumed starts to decrease. So, we might be very happy with the first project on our plate, a little less happy with the second, and then somewhere down the road we get overloaded and our utility starts to decrease. Knowing this, it might be part of our role as project leaders to explain this and help the client to exhaust his utility functions.

By making some additional reasonable assumptions about how we make choices, the theory shows that if we can choose between the projects, then the utility function can be added and multiplied by real numbers so that the utility of a random project can be calculated as a linear combination of the utility of its parts.

In project management the utility of money in the form of cash flow or cost is a common utility function, and is believed by most project leaders to be a nonlinear function. This is taken as a given by many rational choice theories that evolve around the idea of the utility function as a curve in the positive region of the Cartesian co-ordinate system (which makes it appropriate to place utility it in the North-East part of our project ethics matrix (PEM), where it reflects, among other things, the law of diminishing marginal utility. The law of diminishing marginal utility shows that beyond a certain point, money ceases to be useful as an indicator of well-being. This also means that earning and losing money can have radically different impacts on different stakeholders. This nonlinearity of the utility function has profound implications in decision-making processes in project management, where outcomes of choice influence utility through gains or losses of money. It also shows that optimal choice for any given decision depends on the possible outcomes of all other decisions by the same agent in the same time period.

Utility as a measure for well-being has been criticised by Joan Robinson, who claims that it leads to circular logic. 'Utility is the quality in commodities that makes individuals want to buy them, and the fact that individuals want to buy commodities shows that they have utility' (Robinson, 1962: 48). Robinson discusses another weakness of using utility as the sole ethical measure in project management in our case, it becomes all too easy to use it to justify unethical conduct in the name of profit, efficiency, optimising, and so on. This is because the underlying value system will always define the outcome, and is solely based on short-term profit gains which will always justify the outcome in a particular way at the expense of other value-based or ethical considerations.

In modern society, the financial system is set up in such a way that people's excess savings, for example pensions, are often invested as part of an overall portfolio, which may itself involve exchange-traded funds in a basket of companies in a particular index (Dow Jones, Nas 30, S&P 500, and so on). The net effect of this is that the focus of small investors can be largely removed from where their money is ultimately being invested, and, as such, there is a kind of ethical barrier produced by distance from the source. In addition, the marginal utility value of an increase in share price for a number of small investors grouped together in a pension fund, for example, is far greater than, say, for a few very wealthy investors, who are also shareholders. This system produces pressure to maintain short-term profits with quarterly account statements monitored closely and the capacity for more longer-term investments may become more limited.

In this system, the project leader will be the one to implement the will of the executive management and shareholders in a publicly listed company, and, as already illustrated, may be required to execute a project where a conflict of values between different entities is inevitable. The time perspective can be very important in this context, and how it ties in with the compensation of the individuals involved in a project. In the case of the recent explosion and subsequent collapse of the mortgage derivative market, there was a clear misalignment of interests between the short-term compensation received by sellers and facilitators of these products, and the longer-term risks that people would be able to make their mortgage repayments throughout the duration of the loan period. Companies like Bear Stearns and the Icelandic banks (Glitnir, Arion and Landsbanki) which collapsed in 2008, are cases in point. In these examples, investors who bought in at the very high share prices just prior to the collapse lost fortunes, and the majority of employees were left redundant with their reputations tarnished by association. Meanwhile other employees higher up the decision ladder may have been extremely well compensated and able to hold on to their gains, together with other external opportunistic facilitators and favoured investors who were given warning of when to sell (not including those investors that saw through the whole operation and bet on its demise on the basis of their own judgement).

People may argue that experienced investors should have gone into these investments with their eyes open. This is an acceptable point, but in many global cases it is often the taxpayer who is left with the bill to clear up the mess, with institutions being protected by government intervention. This can lead to the build-up of dangerous levels of resentment as taxpayers, who operate on the financial margins, become more impoverished, and the longer-term definition of utility becomes open to question at every level.

Defining utility is notoriously difficult in other sectors, such as energy where the nature of the capital investment, with its complex system of integrated large-scale infrastructure, necessitates long-term perspectives in decision-making, for example on timescales of over 20 years. In addition, the nature of the operations means that the effects of major accidents or other disasters can have far-reaching consequences for the wider population and the environment. Relatively simple decisions made by project leaders in construction and operational managers during an operation can prove vital in damage prevention or limitation and may often come to light in the detailed post-mortems that accompany major incidents. Major human disasters, such as the 1975 flooding of the Banqiao Dam in China, or natural disasters such as the 1989 *Exxon Valdez* oil spill in Alaska, often have as their causes a list of linked weaknesses that come about through a combination of errors at the planning, construction, preparation and operation phases. This can come about as a result of competing values within a project as is evident in the case of the Banqiao Dam. During construction, an eminent hydrologist, Chen Xing, had advised that 12 sluice gates were required for the dam to alleviate the build-up of water behind the dam during extreme flooding events. However, only five sluice gates were included in the original dam on the basis of cost. Chen Xing also made many other notable vehement criticisms of the dam-building policy in China during the Great Leap Forward (1958) and was purged as a 'right-wing opportunist', only to be later reinstated as his warnings invariably turned out to be accurate. This is a common theme in large projects, where the views of technical project leaders can be pitted against the views of those funding the project. So, the definition of utility in these cases can ultimately vary depending on random events, or at least be judged at multiple points in time.

The concept of mutual benefit between project owners and stakeholders has suffered neglect in modern decision-making where utilisation, as narrowly defined by economists, has to be maximised. It can be argued that utility is either incomplete or even irrelevant as a moral concept, or at least that it is not of more significance than other factors such as virtue, duty and rights when it comes to finding justification for our actions. In and of itself, it might also not suffice as a moral measure and needs to be guided or informed by other ethical principles, conscience and/or religious faith.

Utility can be used as an ethical measure as it enables us to quantify decisions, giving backing to the idea that we are making a rational choice – a notion that resonates with the viewpoint of the more traditional economist, engineer and project leader. The problem with the utility function as an ethical measure is that it can become a self-fulfilling prophecy that measures what you can measure, instead of measuring what needs to be measured. The idea that we are able, with certainty, to weigh up all of our ethical options can also create the illusion that we have all the necessary information at our disposal. In the case of the 2011 Fukushima nuclear disaster in Japan, where large amounts of dangerous radiation were released owing to tsunami damage, it seems that, at the planning stages, too much faith was placed on the predictions of technical experts on the natural risk factors in what is a very tectonically active area. The net result is that local stakeholders, such as farmers and fisherman, face a very uncertain future as increased radiation levels in the surrounding land and sea directly affect their future livelihood.

SUCCESS AND VALUE

Despite all that has been said about utility above, the fact remains that we rely on it in our decision-making and it has a strong relevance to project leader practice. The second ethical lens focuses on the outcome, utility or the consequences of our projects. Utility ethics, or utilitarian ethics as it is usually called, originates with David Hume (1711–1776) and was further developed by Jeremy Bentham (1748–1832) and John Stuart Mill (1806–1873). For Bentham there was only one ethical principle. This was utilitarianism, which dictates that we should always choose our actions based on what is best for as many people as possible. If the outcome of our actions is more happiness for more people, then that is what we should do. Through this philosophical idea of utilitarianism, Bentham argued that the right act or policy was that which would do the greatest good for the greatest number of people. Bentham claimed that nature has placed us under two guiding masters: pleasure and pain. He argued that anything good must either be felt as pleasure (or at least an avoidance of pain), and anything bad must be felt as pain (or deprivation of pleasure). Right and wrong, he said, is meaningful only in accordance with the utilitarian principle: *if the project increases the net surplus of pleasure over pain then it is right, and if it decreases it then it is wrong.*

In order to weigh up the ethical consequences of a project and decide whether it is right or wrong to take it on (or certain aspects of it) we must, according to this principle, take into account the pleasures and pains of all stakeholders on an equal basis. In this decision-making process, we must also consider the certainty of the pleasures and pains, their intensity, their longevity, and whether they tend to give rise to further feelings of the same or of the opposite kind. Mill also based his ethics on the maximisation of happiness, which he defined in terms of presence of pleasure and absence of pain. Mill illustrated how utilitarianism is compatible with moral rules and principles, such as justice, honesty, and truthfulness, by arguing that we should not necessarily attempt to calculate before each project whether that particular one will maximise utility (more pleasure than pain) as such. Instead, we should be guided by the fact that a project that falls under a general principle, such as an adherence to certain guiding values, will increase happiness for us as individuals and society. This can be summarised as follows:

- The principle: make sure that the result of your endeavours, as a project leader, will create as much happiness (increase pleasure/lessening pain) for as many as possible.
- Project choice: choose and execute your projects in such a way that they will create as much happiness (more pleasure/less pain) for as many as possible.

A utilitarian project leader would, based on this, claim that the maximisation of utility should be the criterion for all professional demeanours; a strict utilitarian ethicist would claim that the whole organisation of society should be based on utilitarian measures. Society should aim to maximise the total utility of as many individuals as possible and aim for 'the greatest happiness for the greatest number of people'. In the ethical theory of John Rawls (1921–2002), who aimed to combine utilitarianism and rights ethics (see the chapter on rights ethics), it is suggested that society should aim at maximising the utility of those individuals who had initially been receiving the minimum amount of utility, namely the poor and the needy. We are not sure if there are too many project or programme managers who would take Rawls' notion of professional responsibility as a sole reference point, though the basic idea is illuminating and worth consideration.

Another aspect of assessing the utility value of projects is the legal viewpoint. This has always been an important responsibility of the project leader, as others can make legitimate claims on the basis of negligence in performing one's duties. However, one also needs to be increasingly aware of the growing culture of litigation, whereby opportunistic individuals are on the lookout for potential rewards. Originating especially in the US, but now becoming more widespread, this culture has steadily grown over the last few decades and sophisticated methods may be used. The utility value of applying best practice in project management is therefore very high in order to avoid any potential pitfalls in this regard. Legal action taken against entities, particularly individuals and small companies, can be extremely costly, paralysing and ultimately too much to recover from without dramatic consequences.

EFFICIENCY AND EFFECTIVENESS

Project success is extensively discussed in the project management literature. As mentioned in the introduction, it is traditional in the field of project management to discuss project success in terms of the 'Iron Triangle', sometimes called the project management triangle or triple constraint. In this model, quality, time and cost are interconnected in a graphical representation, indicating that there must be a balance between those three dimensions. In other words, you cannot have it all. If quality is what you aim for, you may have to make sacrifices in cost and time. If time is of greatest concern, sacrifices may have to be made in terms of quality and cost, and so on.

Even though the Iron Triangle is something of a simplification, it is a simplification with great practical value. It is easy to explain and is widely known and accepted within the project management community. In recent years, however, project management practitioners and researchers have given more attention to other aspects of project success that are not in any way represented in the simple Iron Triangle: themes relating to people, the impact on the environment, the actual output of the project including its basic purpose and its connection to the organisational strategy at large.

Here it is helpful to introduce the concepts of (1) project success and (2) project management success, which also brings time into the equation. Project management success is short-term, and has to do with the ways a project is prepared and managed, how well processes are applied and how well the project leader and his team perform during the project life cycle. Project success is a more long-term concept and asks whether the output of the project has been of use and of benefit in terms of utility of some sort. This question cannot be answered during the project life cycle but has to be answered when the impact, consequence or outcome of the project has been actualised or revealed. It might, in fact, take a long time before a complete answer to this question can be established.

One consequence of making a distinction between project success and project management success is that it makes sense to talk about a project being successful in terms of project management, but unsuccessful as a project. An example could be a project where plans were made and carried out using the correct procedures, leading to the delivery of an output at the correct cost and meeting a time deadline. From a limited viewpoint, this would mean that all managerial actions of the project were conducted according to ethical standards. We see from this that not only is the time perspective rather short, but also the ethical scope is narrowed down and limited to the inner life of the project. Here, for instance, the question would be whether the stakeholder analysis was well conducted, and not whether the project actually impacted negatively on other stakeholders, as such.

With regard to project success we are faced with a different scenario. Here we are necessarily dealing with a longer period of time and a wider perspective. Traditionally, the ethical consideration has been limited to the question: has the project brought the expected outcomes to the project owner, or not? If the project fails in this case, the reason for the failure might either be due to failure in the project management success or as a consequence of events or forces that are not within the control of the project management.

As we are discussing ethics, we should ask what would be sufficient success criteria and also necessary success criteria for projects. Who is to determine the outcome of a project if it has the expected properties and brings the expected benefits? Traditionally, project leaders would claim that this is a rather simple question to answer: it will suffice if the real project outcome meets the expected project outcomes of the project owner, client or project organisation. But is it necessarily so? Might there be other necessary outcomes that we need to consider? Ethically speaking the answer to this question is definitely yes: the sufficient condition would be to meet the expectations of the owner, but the necessary conditions would be to meet the demands of ethical standards.

We come, therefore, back to the concept of value, which, in a commercial context, is usually defined as the price someone is willing to pay for a product or service. It is thus something that can be maximised by increasing revenue and reducing cost, or in ethical utilitarianism as the rationale between benefits (pleasure) and cost (pain). Usually project success is defined by increasing utility or value for the project owner, and preferably delivering an output at the lowest cost and without sacrificing what was expected.

In modern times, however, and with increased understanding of how our project outcomes might have an impact on both society and the environment, it is becoming a necessary condition for real project success to reflect the wider picture in the project environment. From this standpoint, the value for the client is only part of the equation and cannot be optimised no matter what; other interests are at stake and must also be taken into account. We will discuss this in more detail in the chapter on rights.

UTILITY AND PROJECT MANAGEMENT SUCCESS

Project management success can also be defined in terms of excellence. Harrington (1996) argued that 10 per cent of organisations deliver excellent results, whereas over 50 per cent of organisations are below average in this regard. Examples of business organisations that are believed to have built up a reputation for excellence might include Hewlett Packard, Motorola, McDonald's, Xerox, Boeing and Toyota. The quest for the methods they employ that are likely to enhance excellence in utilitarian outcome can be found in books such as *In Search of Excellence* by Peters and Waterman (1982), *Total Organisational Excellence* by John Oakland (1999) and *Good To Great* by Jim Collins (2001).

Excellence in management is usually associated with good leadership, efficient processes and first-rate delivery. These are reflected, for instance, in the European Foundation of Quality Management (EFQM) model which are the criteria for the European Quality Award.

The International Project Management Association (IPMA) has defined project management excellence, and their approach to this is evident in what they emphasise as important in their annual Project Excellence Award. The IPMA evaluation focuses on three basic success criteria: project management, project results, innovation and learning. Special attention is paid to (1) Project management success: project objectives, leadership, people, resources and process; and (2) Project success: results for customers, results for the people involved, results for other stakeholders, performance and project results in terms of utility. The IPMA application brochure for the reward addresses specifically the concept of social responsibility under the theme of criteria. Their application brochure, which specifically addresses the nominee selection criteria, states that 'every excellent company needs to understand that it can never make optional decisions if they are isolated from the environment. Ethics and social responsibility play an important part in all decisions' (see application brochure, the highest international honours for excellent project performance, IPMA – International Project Excellence Award, Assessment based on the project excellence model; see www.ipma.ch, Aug, 2011).

According to this project excellence model, good project success equals or exceeds the expectations of clients, people and other parties involved. Excellence is also doing things better than they have been done before and manifests itself in an outcome that is difficult to repeat and will be remembered.

UTILITY AND PROJECT SUCCESS

The concept of project success still remains ambiguous, and notions of management success can often come across as rather masculine and military in nature. For example, Shenhar *et al.* (2003) mention project success in terms of (gaining) advantage, superiority, victory, accomplishment, achievement, and added value. Given the wide range of considerations and motivations, project success is probably one of those concepts within project management that is least agreed upon.

If we remind ourselves of Aristotle's notion of theoretical and practical wisdom, both project management researchers (concerned with theoretical wisdom) and project leaders (concerned with practical wisdom) have struggled to identify the managerial variables that are critical to success. Typical questions within the discourse are: should project leaders who meet budget and schedule constraints, but do not meet customer needs and requirements, be deemed as successful? Or, are project leaders, where the outcome is a product of good quality but that has no demand or cannot be put on the market due to regulatory, legal or ethical constraints, a success?

These are difficult questions to find generalised answers to and the fact remains that the project management literature does not provide a consistent definition of the term success. Standardised definitions of project successes are vague and there is no absolute and universally accepted methodology of measuring them. Hence project success is usually defined in quite broad terms.

Derived from what we already know about utility theories, we recognise that project success will inevitably have to have both subjective and objective measures; it will also inevitably mean different things to different people. Some work has been done on conceptualising project and project management success (Jugdev and Müller, 2005). Over time, concepts of success have evolved from seeing project success as being merely technically correct for the providing organisation to seeing how the project interfaces with the client organisation and flows from internal and external factors (Pinto and Slevin, 1988b). Projects can consist of a series of project goals that can be seen as building blocks towards achieving a targeted business objective ('effect-goal') that arises from the productive use of the project outcome (Wenell, 2000). In ethical terms, while it would be desirable if project leaders took responsibility for these more long-term objectives, it is often not possible due to the temporary nature of the project and the time gap between project delivery and the impact of business results.

PROJECT SUCCESS AND PROJECT MANAGEMENT SUCCESS

How to determine whether a project as such is a success or a failure when, for example, there are delays in its completion? De Wit (1988) was among the first to recognise that there is a difference between project success and project management success. The importance of the distinction is that successful project management will inevitably contribute to project success, whereas the project management might not stop a project deliverable from failing to succeed. Baccarini (1999) claims that the literature on project management also tends to fuse two other separate dimensions of project success: product success and project management success.

Project management success focuses on fulfilling the cost, time and quality managerial criteria. Project success, however, deals with the outcome of the project's final deliverable, such as the project goals, project purpose and the satisfaction of stakeholders. The classical examples used to illustrate this are the Sydney Opera House and Project Orion. First the famous Sydney Opera House, with its aesthetically pleasing and very novel design, is widely considered a grand example of project success. Yet, from a project management perspective, it was a spectacular failure, as its cost went from the estimated (1959) US$7 million to over US$100 million, when finished 14 years later (1973) (*Architecture Week*, 2003). What was the collective happiness/pain ratio for this project? Even though the project management success has been judged as very low, the impact and the activities within it might have created much more utility than its cost. This does not justify the inefficiency in its construction, but it might be something to consider.

The second example is a project that is perceived as a project management success but a failure from a project success viewpoint. Project Orion was the name given to the development of Kodak's new Advantix photographic system, which was reputedly very well managed from a project management perspective. PMI recognised it as the 1997 International Project of the Year, with *Business Week* selecting the system as one of the best new products of 1996 (Adams, 1998). However, Kodak's stock price dropped hugely after the introduction of the Advantix system, 'in part as it failed to anticipate the accelerating switch to digital photography' (Bandler, 2003).

Project success might, therefore, be a rather subjective notion as it can mean different things to different people (Liu and Walker, 1998). Different users and stakeholders might perceive the outcome of the project differently and Shenhar *et al.* (2002) suggest three reasons for this difference in perception: (1) the universalistic managerial approach, where all projects are assumed to be similar; (2) the subjective nature of the success and/or vaguely defined success measures; and (3) the limited number of managerial variables examined.

Munns and Bjeirmi (1996) believe this difference in perception will continue to exist as long as the distinction between project success and project management success is not properly established. Project management success is oriented towards the planning and control of the short-term life of the project development and delivery. Project success is long-term in nature and stretches towards the actual objective or product that the project delivers. Project management success focuses on the quality of the management process and its impact on the success criteria defined in accordance with the Iron Triangle, including the preparation and execution phases in the project life cycle. The other part of project success relates to the overall effect of the project's deliverable or service, and is referred to as 'product success' (Baccarini, 1999). Therefore, a project can be viewed as being successful even if the Iron Triangle criteria are not met. Munns and Bjeirmi (1996) agree on this and illustrate it as follows (Figure 3.2).

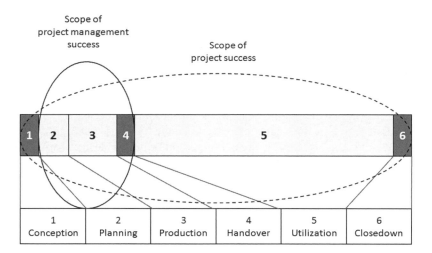

Figure 3.2   The scope of success within the project life cycle (Munns and Bjeirmi, 1996)

Source: Reprinted from *International Journal of Project Management*, Munns and Bjeirmi, April 1996, 'The Role of Project Management in Achieving Project Success', pp. 81–87, June 2012 with permission from Elsevier.

Usually, the project management team would be regarded as mainly aiming at a successful completion of the handover phase of the project (phase 4); the client, on the other hand, is concerned with all the phases. *Project management success* spans phases 1–4 but *project success* spans all the phases (Munns and Bjeirmi 1996). Project success is naturally *utilitarian* in nature, and the distinction between project management success and project success is not just about terminology. It defines the establishment of appropriate methods for managing the project life-cycle and for the selection of suitable measurements (Bryde, 2005). In our definition of success it is crucial to understand the importance of those success factors or inputs to the project management system that have an influence on the outcome.

The PMBOK of the Project Management Institute breaks the project life cycle up into three main phases: (1) initial implementation; (2) intermediate execution, and (3) final handover. The literature on project success mainly focuses on the implementation or execution phases (Lim and Mohamed, 1999), probably because the implementation phase is typically the longest phase and the phase that is most resource consuming (PMI, 2000).

PROJECT SUCCESS CRITERIA AND PROJECT SUCCESS FACTORS

It is also important to identify the variables that define project success. According to Wateridge (1995), successful projects need at least two project success components to be clearly described and agreed upon by all involved. These are (1) the project success criteria of users and sponsors, and (2) the project success factors required to deliver the success criteria.

The success criteria become the benchmark for measuring success or failure, and the success factors are the management inputs and systems that lead to project success (Cooke-Davies, 2002). Westerveld (2003) linked success criteria and success factors together in his Project Excellence Model. It is based on the EFQM business excellence model and aims to help project leaders deal with large and complex projects. The model is, furthermore, based on the assumption that in order to manage a project successfully, the project organisation has to focus on result areas containing project success criteria and organisational areas containing critical success factors. Figure 3.3 illustrates both the content and the context of the model.

Westerveld claims that the Project Excellence Model can be applied in different project stages and situations, and that it can be used for setting up, managing, and evaluating projects. The term 'Key performance indicators' (APM, 2000) is often used interchangeably with the term 'Project success criteria.'

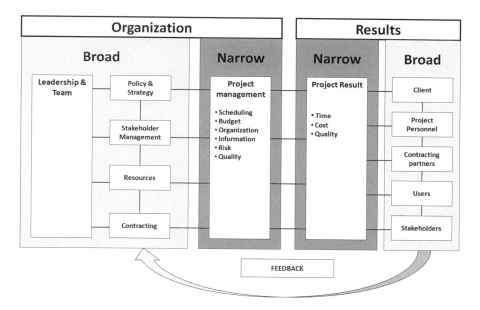

Figure 3.3   The Project Excellence Model (Westerveld, 2003)
Source: Reprinted from *International Journal of Project Management*, Westerveld, August 2003, The Project Excellence Model ®: Linking Success Criteria and Critical Success, pp. 411–418, June 2012 with permission from Elsevier.

There are also the *Critical Success Factor lists* (*CSF*) that define the 'elements required for creating an environment where projects are managed consistently with excellence' (Kerzner, 1987: 32). Associated with this is the increased focus on the stakeholders' and customers' satisfaction as an indicator of successful project outcome (Lim and Mohamed, 1999), though users are generally more concerned with satisfaction completion than completion as a criterion (Munns and Bjeirmi, 1996). Quality is often defined in terms of satisfying users' needs or as the utility gained by users. Success for the user will be oriented towards long-term utilisation of the project deliverable rather than anything that has to do with project management success.

When executing the project, the project team is concerned with the project game and its principles. They might have little or no direct contact with the user. The user might also remain unaware of the project management processes and its successes (Munns and Bjeirmi, 1996). The emphasis in this case is that it is the duty of the project leader to deliver something useful for the owner. We will discuss duty in more detail in the next chapter.

What then are the success factors? Pinto and Prescott (1990) use anecdotes and single case studies, while other writers indicate that excellence in project success can be measured within time, cost and performance/quality constraints (Kerzner, 1987). Such use of metrics, however, can be misleading if the expected outcomes for the end-users are not met. Jugdev and Müller (2005) discuss how success can be described as a single measure for the project as a whole, instead of multiple measures over the life cycle (in other words the project is either a success or a failure) and what the different implications of this can be.

Raz, Senhar and Dvir (2002) look at how the use of risk management relates to project success. They found that risk management seems, overall, to add to project success, but that it is more applicable to higher-risk projects, and that it mainly influences time and budget rather than performance and specification. Shenhar *et al.* (2002) tried to refine the search for project success factors and to identify project-specific managerial variables that are critical to successful industrial projects. Two of their major findings strongly suggest that successful project management is influenced by a wide spectrum of variables and also that project success factors are indeed contingent upon the specific type of project. As we can see, the list of project success factors is far from universal.

Dvir *et al.* (2003) have examined the relationship between planning efforts and project success. They concluded that project success is insensitive to the level of implementation of management processes due to the relatively high quality of modern computerised management tools and project management training. On the other hand, project success is sensitive to the level of definition of requirements and development of technical specifications. Additionally, there is a positive relationship between the amount of effort invested in defining project goals and project success as it is seen in by the end-user. So if we want a good outcome, no effort should be spared in the initial stage of a project to get the necessary initial feedback from the client, customer and end-user to properly guide the direction of the project.

Dvir and Lechler (2004), have also looked at the interactions between three project planning variables for the project outcome: (1) the quality of planning, (2) goal changes, and (3) plan changes. They found that the positive total effect of the quality of planning can be almost completely overridden by the negative effects of goal changes. The quality of planning, therefore, positively affects both efficiency and customer satisfaction, while changes do the opposite and compromise the project outcome. Dvir (2005) also examined the relationship between planning and preparing the project for transfer of its outcome to end-users. He concluded that projects contracted for a specific customer should devote considerable effort to planning and preparing in advance of the handover of the project outcome to its final users. Customer involvement in all phases of the project can strongly contribute to the project success and customer participation in the development process and final user preparations have the highest impact on project success.

MULTIDIMENSIONAL CRITICAL SUCCESS FACTOR FRAMEWORKS

No matter how we look it, it is clear that good project outcomes are multi-dimensional phenomena that cannot be assessed only by single-, two- or three-dimensional measures. This is confirmed by Shenhar and Wideman (1996), who defined the following four primary categories of successful outcomes of a project: (1) internal project objectives (efficiency during the project), (2) benefit to customer (effectiveness in the short term), (3) current contribution (in the medium term) and (4) future opportunity (in the long term). They created a classification for projects to assess the correlation between term-based primary success criteria and types of projects. They classified project data into four project types, namely (1) established technology (Type A), (2) mostly established technology (Type B), (3) advanced technology (Type C) and (4) highly advanced technology (Type D). It turned out that the relative importance of the different categories of success varied with technological uncertainty. More specifically, the importance of time and budget constraints is reduced with increasing uncertainty, while the impact of project outcome on the customer increases when moving from established technology to higher technology with higher uncertainty. The four primary categories of project success, the four project types and, potentially, the three levels of project management complexity, do, indeed, provide a valuable framework for developing Principal Success Criteria.

Shenhar et al. (1997) introduced a multi-dimensional and multi-observational framework to identify four universal dimensions of project success, namely (1) project efficiency, (2) impact on customers, (3) business and direct success and (4) preparing for the future. Meeting design goals (time, budget and performance) was not a homogeneous dimension. Time and budget comprised one resource-related dimension, whereas meeting specifications related to customer satisfaction. Success also varies over the course of the project and product life cycle. The study placed customer satisfaction as the first criterion for overall project success and the Iron Triangle as the second. The multi-dimensional concept is further discussed in a paper by Shenhar, Dvir, Levy and Maltz (2001) where the strategic perspective is emphasised still more, and projects are presented as powerful strategic weapons. The paper demonstrates how these dimensions should be addressed during the project's definition, planning, and execution phases, and provides a set of guidelines for project leaders and senior managers.

In an interdisciplinary study by Dvir et al. (2006) the focus was on the relationships between three aspects of projects, namely (1) project types (profiles), (2) project leader personalities and (3) project success. The hypothesis was that if the type and nature of a project were matched to the personality of a project leader, then they would be more successful. Even though the study did not offer much support for this hypothesis, the authors acknowledge that a fit between project leaders' personalities and the types of projects they manage might be crucial for project success.

Case 5 – Ayize and Fly

Ayize is a project leader in charge of improving customer service projects for an airline company that operates in a very fast changing and mobile market. The project 'Fly' has recently introduced an automated telephone response system for customers in order to reduce staff costs. The labour union has reacted strongly to the action and there has been negative coverage in the media. Whilst the desired cost reduction has been achieved, the level of customer complaints rose dramatically as soon as the new system was introduced. A small percentage of customers have said that they will never fly with the airline again, while a much larger percentage have said that if they had a proper choice (the airline is currently cheaper than its competitors), they would switch to using their competitors immediately.

Questions:

- What are the ethical concerns in this case?
- What are the competing values in this case?
- How would you define utility in this case?
- What would you advise Ayize to do?

REINVENTING PROJECT MANAGEMENT

In *Reinventing Project Management* Shenhar and Dvir (2007) state that 'every operational process begins as a project that puts things in motion' and that there is a tendency among high level managers to look at project budgets as a cost rather than an investment. They also state that even though the conventional project management body of knowledge might form a good basis for training and initial learning, it might not suffice for addressing the complexities of project management. To meet this demand, therefore, they made a framework based on the following questions: (1) Can we help project teams make the right assessment before presenting their project proposal to top management? (2) Can we show executives how to ask the right questions and foresee danger before they make a commitment to a project, and before it is too late? (3) Can we guide project teams in adapting their project management style to the circumstances, environment and tasks?

The model was called the adaptive project management framework. It aimed at enabling managers to understand project management better and to offer a more success-focused and flexible model. It is a multi-dimensional model for assessing and planning project success beyond the Iron Triangle of time, cost and quality, and assumes that the project leader is responsible for the multidimensional outcome related metrics of project success. The model takes into consideration the strategic and tactical aspects of project performance in both the short and the long term. It also considers the points of view of different project stakeholders, including customers and business. We believe, however, that they have only used vague ethical considerations and the ones accounted for are all concealed within the utility-based measures deployed. The model is a diamond-shaped framework within which to analyse the expected benefits and risks of a project and to offer a set of rules and behaviours for each project type. The aim is to help managers distinguish between projects according to four dimensions: (1) novelty, (2) technology, (3) complexity and (4) pace – and these four dimensions are defined as the essentials of successful projects. Novelty represents the uncertainty of the project's goals and/or uncertainty in the market. Technology represents the level of technological uncertainty associated with the project or how much new technology is needed. Complexity refers to the complexity of the product, the task and the project organisation. Pace represents the urgency of the project; how much time there is to complete the job (Shenhar and Dvir, 2007).

> *In our survey we asked participants to respond to statements regarding utility ethics in project management: 65% disagreed with the idea that it is only justifiable to start a project if it increases accumulated happiness of all interest groups, whereas 28% agreed. 54% were neutral towards a statement saying that 'all my projects increase the happiness of my project team'. 43% were neutral and 28% agreed when responding to the statement 'all my projects have increased the happiness within my organisation'. 36% were neutral and 51% agreed that 'all my projects have increased the happiness of my customers'. 58% were neutral, 15% neutral and 24% agreed that 'all my projects have increased the happiness of my society'. 47% were neutral, 29% agreed and 18% disagreed with the statement 'I choose and execute my projects in such a way as to create as much happiness as possible for as many as possible' (Sigurðarson, 2009).*

The questions that could be directed at utility ethics are: is it only justifiable to start a project if it increases the accumulated happiness of all interest groups? The project team? The organisation? The customer? Society? As we noted in the previous discussion of virtue ethics, utility ethics is also somewhat subjective in nature. In this case, it is about where we draw the line as to what groups we are measuring the utility values for, and also what the successful criteria are in each case.

We can see from the discussion so far that, according to a pure utilitarian view of the world, only pleasure, happiness or well-being, are worthy objectives to pursue. The aim, therefore, of all conduct, projects, programmes and portfolios, should be to increase happiness or well-being in the long run. The justification of an action is defined by the notion that if the project increases happiness in the long run within society, it is justifiable and should be done. If this is not the case, it is not justifiable and should not be done. Each and every project owner has a role to play here. However, it is not only the project owner who has a role, because, as project leaders, we are also active agents in the actualising process.

A problem arises where there is a divergence from an objective and the actions to deal with it form a project within a project which will take us from the current undesired situation to a new desired position. If this happens, then the client is closer to a desired objective and the outcome will be an increase in their happiness. Engineering sciences and affiliated disciplines, such as project and quality management, apply knowledge to identify a particular problem. There are many established methods for this including using a systematic process of elimination similar to how an electrician may identify a short circuit. Once identified, solutions need to be found that are compatible with all the related aspects of the project and which do not lead to unintended consequences. This type of problem solving can become very complex in fields such as aeronautical engineering, where there is a very high level of interdependency between variables. This is also the case in other fields, such as central banking, where very small changes in policy may have very exaggerated effects on the real economy and must be approached very carefully.

Utilitarian ethics talks about society rather than individuals. We could then argue that if one person is happier than before and the solution does not inflict pain upon others, then this is good and well justified. In this case, decision-making should be very simple, and, if the solution is also efficient and effective, then there is even more happiness. If the solution does not have an impact on others, then the benefits of the outcomes could just add up to the sum of happiness for all of the individual solutions, whereby one gets the sum increase of happiness within society. Things are rarely that simple! The problem with this approach is that it assumes that our projects have non-interfering variables. However, when we decide to interfere with something, we could end up with a very different situation. Therefore, more consideration is needed at the early stages of projects, as solutions – or projects – can also inflict pain upon others. No project is an island and totally independent from other projects. To give an example, we could think of the social impact of a bridge, the impact of the bicycle, the impact of building power plants and the exploitation of oil for consumption on nature. Projects such as these interfere with other projects, and with society, and can have both positive and negative unintended consequences. Many large projects such as gas pipelines may be built for very sound economic reasons, as economies of scale in a normal functioning market should lead to lower costs for the end-user. This can lead to over-dependence on external entities, however, and if they later develop a more aggressive stance to extract more compensation, one can be left with little option but to accept the new conditions if other avenues have been closed off. Even implied threats are very important in this type of situation and the scope for alternative decision-making can be increasingly reduced.

The problem with the utilitarian justification for a project is that the solution often has an impact on others beyond the client, and it can have an (sometimes totally unexpected) impact far into the future. It can, for instance, drastically increase the unhappiness of someone within society and also decrease happiness in society at large. Public perception is very important in this case as is the ability of the public to be able to understand and run their own internal simulations as to how a project will affect them. This issue is critical to success: it is not enough to do good, but it must be recognised as such.

An example where difficulty is widely encountered in this regard is in the field of biotechnology and, in particular, in the use of technologies such as genetic modification. Here, scientists' attempts to explain the risks involved have yet to convince many people. This is despite the fact that a large body of research has been built up to back up their claims of safety. It is not possible for the normal person to understand what is going on at the molecular level and, as such, they are reliant on the views of experts filtered through the media for a simplified understanding of how the system operates. The slant taken in the media is, of course, important, but people have their own innate understanding of human nature and will naturally always question the motivation of those promoting a concept and ask whether scientists have fully thought through the consequences of their actions. The public might become suspicious of a project and this could, in the view of the project supporters, be based on making unfounded connections between previous negative outcomes in completely different disciplines. This is a fact of life that has to be dealt with by both sides so that solutions can be reached.

It is important to note that any potential solution needs to fulfil standards and methods that the field has deemed as appropriate or that is bound by laws and regulations. Sometimes special consideration is required before the solution is used. An example of how utility measures have functioned in this regard is reflected in how flight security has changed over the last decade since the terrorist attacks on the United States on 11 September, 2001. Here, the trade-off is between, on the one hand, the imposition of more intrusive security measures with consequent effects on people's rights to privacy, longer queuing times and higher costs associated with extra security equipment and personnel, and, on the other hand, the knowledge that the likelihood of similar events recurring has been greatly reduced owing to these extra security measures.

In summary, utility ethics is a widely cited approach in modern project management, and while it takes us far, our approach as project leaders needs to consider carefully how we assign utility value to our projects, as well as what the opportunity costs of pursuing a particular mode of action are. In order to help with this process we have included below a list of questions that should be asked by project leaders at the outset of their projects:

- How strong is utilitarianism as a justification for project action?
- Is project management success or project success more important, or are they both equally important?
- Who are the principal beneficiaries of the project and how?
- Who are the secondary beneficiaries of the project and how?
- Who might suffer as a result of the project and how?
- Does the client know their needs and expectations?
- What are the utility values that can be measured? What utility values should be measured?
- What are the opportunity costs associated with the project and can they be measured?
- How do you as a project leader, communicate your utilitarian approach to all the relevant stakeholders?

CHAPTER 4

PROCESS-ORIENTED PROJECT ETHICS: DUTY ETHICS

Never let your sense of morals prevent you from doing what is right.
Isaac Asimov (1920–1992), Russian writer and scientist

> Fully informed and with a clear conscience, are you sure that the project process (everything that happens in the project) is managed in such a way that it could define a universal principle with regard to how projects should be managed?

DUTY AND THE RULES OF THE GAME

The professional project leader is faced with many demanding managerial duties. Fulfilling some might be easy and pleasurable, but others might be demanding and difficult. The management of a complex project is a mission that entails a variety of responsibilities which can either be well defined or not so easily recognised at the outset, and sometimes the duties can be conflicting. With these observations in mind, what predefines the duties of the project leader? Who defines these duties? How do we deal with situations if these responsibilities clash?

The third ethical principle that will be explored is the project ethics of duty. The concept of duty derives from the word 'due', as in 'it is your due to …' meaning 'owing'. It comes from the French verb *devoir* meaning 'to have to', which points to obligation and necessity. In Latin, the term relates to *debere* and *debitum*, but the associated English term 'debt' conveys a sense of moral commitment to someone or something, as when a borrower owes something to a lender. In short, the concept of duty refers to things that we cannot choose to do or not to do, but to the things *that we have to do* no matter what, because it is our absolute obligation. The moral commitment, according to this definition, results not in speculation on moral conduct, but on action only, and cannot be reduced to a matter of passive feeling or mere recognition of moral responsibility. Our duty is therefore the inevitable responsibility to do something rather than not, or not to do something rather than do it. Further, duty demands moral action from the individual more than anything else. Each individual has responsibilities and it is his or her duty to act in accordance with them.

The illustration we use to portray duty ethics shows a man standing on a path (Figure 4.1). The dot that represents the ethical stand is not at the end of the path but 'here and now' along the way. The justification for action or no action is not based on result but on the principles that define the path. It presents a principle to be followed along the path, no matter the presumed outcome.

One does not have to read far into project management professional standards and competence baselines to see indications of what the authors define as the duties of the professional project leader. Some examples of this might include the duty to ensure that projects are well defined, carefully planned and orchestrated; the duty to review all planning carefully and to set measurable goals for time, cost, quality and customer satisfaction; the duty to work in the best interests of the project owner.

Figure 4.1   Duty is the straight path of uncompromising obligation

In our survey we tried to elicit project leaders' sense of responsibility to see if they believe that they comply with the above duties by asking for their response to the following statements:

- A project plan is made for all projects that I am a part of.
- Project plans are always reviewed before execution in my projects.
- Measurable goals for time are always defined in my projects.
- Measurable goals for cost are always defined in my projects.
- Measurable goals for quality are always defined in my projects.
- Measurable goals for customer satisfaction are always defined in my projects.

The responses were as follows: 61 per cent agreed (or strongly agreed) that a project plan is made for all projects that they are a part of, while 29 per cent disagreed (or strongly disagreed); 53 per cent agreed (or strongly agreed) that the plans are always reviewed before being put into execution, while 31 per cent disagreed (or strongly disagreed); 78 per cent agreed (or strongly agreed) that measurable goals for time are always defined in their projects, while 14 per cent disagreed (or strongly disagreed); 69 per cent agreed (or strongly agreed) that measurable goals for cost are always defined in their projects, while 17 per cent disagreed (or strongly disagreed); 71 per cent agreed (or strongly agreed) that measurable goals for quality are always defined in their projects, while 13 per cent disagreed (or strongly disagreed); 64 per cent agreed (or strongly agreed) that measurable goals for customer satisfaction are always defined in their projects, while 20 per cent disagreed (or strongly disagreed). (Sigurðarson, 2009).

The above results give a narrow project-focused indication of how duty is regarded by project leaders. A rough summary could be that at the outset, two-thirds of the respondents consciously plan their duties and how they will measure their successes in this regard.

Duty ethics is in many ways more straightforward than either virtue ethics or utility ethics, as the path to follow in decision-making is more likely to be well signposted – there tends to be fewer distractions. As a result, one need not spend too long considering the consequences of one's actions, the merits for themselves, or the impact for the many. One's actions are only based on what is deemed to be obligatory. Duty project ethics is, therefore, focused solely on the individual sense of responsibility, no matter what the consequences. It does not necessarily suggest that living a life of duty precludes good living, but it does simply imply that duty can involve a sacrifice of either immediate or long-term self-interest.

In his work 'On Duty' (*De officiis*) (Cicero, 2001:44), the Roman philosopher Marcus Tullius Cicero suggested that sense of duty come from four different sources: from being a human being; from our particular place in life, such as within our family, our country or our job; from our personality and character traits; and from our own moral expectations of ourselves.

Professionally, the idea of obligation to serve or give something in return relates to the concept of duty. Some examples of this are the services performed by clerics towards their congregation, the services carried out by soldiers, by servants to their masters, or employees to their organisation. Some ethicists have also argued that mankind as such has been assigned duties towards animals, nature and God or gods. But duty as a moral ideal is also questionable and it has been debated whether the idea of duty serves well as a tool for normative ethics. While many assert that every human being and the human race have a special duty towards others, animals and nature, some authors have absolutely rejected the idea that there is any sense of duty that has, in itself, intrinsic validity.

CRITICAL SUCCESS FACTOR FRAMEWORKS

How can we further extend the notion of duty to project leadership? One way to do so is to discuss duty in terms of product life cycle phases and the Critical Success Factor (CSF) frameworks that were developed by Jugdev and Müller (2005). The method differs somewhat from older approaches, where the duty of the project leader in terms of success was more stakeholder-dependent, and focused narrowly on the interactions between the internal and recipient organisation (Kerzner, 1987; Lester, 1998).

De Wit (1988) can be said to have broadened this notion of project leadership duties by designing a project success framework that stakeholders, project objectives and the project management took into consideration. For him, there are two components to project success: the success criteria that have been defined, and the manner in which project objectives are met.

Kerzner (1987) discussed CSFs and the associated sense of duty for project leaders by stating that project success criteria should be extended to projects, project management, the project organisation, senior management and the project environment. To some degree, different things matter at different times, though conceptualisation, planning, execution and termination, and the relative importance of CSFs varies over the course the project life cycle (Pinto and Covin, 1989). One of the most important success factors throughout all four phases of the life cycle is the maintenance of the project mission. This insight shows that the project mission is one of the fundamental duties of the project leader.

Some Critical Success Factor Frameworks are common to all projects regardless of their type, while others are type specific. Furthermore, project success is multi-dimensional and perceived project success can be seen as consisting of three conceptually and statistically distinct factors: (1) the implementation process, (2) the perceived 'value' of the project; and (3) the client satisfaction (Pinto and Prescott 1990). These aspects are the responsibility of the dutiful project leader.

Morris and Hough (1987) give an insight into project duties with their idea that seven forces determine project success: (1) to try one's best to manage the external context of the project including project sponsorship; (2) to be well aware of the external political, economic, social, technical, legal and environmental (PESTLE) factors that might have an impact on the project; (3) to have, and to ensure that others also have, the attitudes reflecting the importance that needs to be attached to the project, and manage the support given to it at all levels of management; (4) to clearly define all indications of what is needed for the project to be accomplished, and design and use the appropriate technology to achieve this; (5) to find and manage the right people for the task, show leadership and make good teamwork possible; (6) to use the right systems for planning, reporting and controlling; and (7) to foster a good organisational connection between different roles, responsibilities and all contractual relationships.

Morris and Hough (1987) also agree that project leadership duties should include managing: (1) attitudes, (2) project definition, (3) external factors, (4) finance, (5) organisation, (6) contract strategy, (7) schedule, (8) communications, (9) control, (10) human qualities and (11) resource management. They also go on to state that any notion of project success has both subjective and objective sides, that success varies across the project and product life cycle, and that various stakeholders are involved.

We could also try to define the project leader's responsibility by using Pinto's and Covin's '10 CSF' list (Pinto and Covin, 1989; Pinto and Mantel, 1990; Pinto and Slevin, 1987, 1988a, 1989). According to this list, the project leader should see his or her duty in terms of (1) sustaining the project mission, (2) managing top management support, (3) keeping a close track of the project schedule/plan, (4) consulting the client, (5) finding the right people to work on the project, (6) using the best technology to support the project, (7) ensuring there is acceptance by the client, (8) guaranteeing monitoring and feedback, (9) keeping channels of communication open, and (10) having the expertise to deal with troubleshooting. One could also look to Turner (1999) for help in determining the duties that come into play in project management. His approach builds on Morris and Hough (1987), using both subjective and objective criteria.

Cleland and Ireland (2002) examine project leader duties from two perspectives: first, in terms of the project leader's duty to aim for and reach technical project performance objectives – for example time, cost and scope – and second, in terms of the duty to align the contribution of the project to the strategic mission of the organisation. The duty of the project management would be to mirror both perspectives and to guarantee both. Fortune and White (2006) view project leader duties in terms of the Formal Systems Model (FSM). According to this model, the responsibility of the project leader is to aim for the CSFs, while at the same time avoiding the problems associated with them. These models differ from the CSF models in the following ways: firstly, that inter-relationships between factors are at least as important as the individual factors themselves, though the Critical Success Factors approach might not, when narrowly orchestrated, provide a mechanism for taking account of these inter-relationships; and, secondly, that 'The factor approach tends to view implementation as a static process instead of a dynamic phenomenon, and ignores the potential for a factor to have varying levels of importance at different stages of the implementation process' (Fortune and White, 2006).

Procaccino and Verner (2006) studied a group of software development project leaders to see how they, *in reality*, defined success in their duties. Surprisingly, only one of the three factors traditionally used to measure success according to the Iron Triangle (cost, time, quality) was widely considered. This was quality. The other two criteria, completing a project on time and within budget, did not, in fact, appear to have much relevance for many of the respondents. This may reflect the fact that much software development is not capital intensive and that the programming aspects of these projects have to be entirely error-free before there will be any output, thus influencing the views of project leaders within this field accordingly.

Case 6 – Natasha and Ethilibrium

Natasha, an established Australian musical composer and experienced film producer, has received a large advance payment from a film production company to complete a film score as part of a year-long project, a new film with the working title 'Ethilibrium'. Natasha is a shareholder and owns 50 per cent of the film production company. Her advance payment includes the money required to actualise the project, book studio time and session musicians, as well as providing generous personal expenses. On the basis of discussions with friends, however, Natasha has decided to become involved in property investment, as she believes the year-on-year double-digit growth in house prices is due to continue for the foreseeable future. As a result, she has used a considerable portion of the initial advance received to get a leveraged loan from the bank, which she has subsequently invested in the property market. Now, however, six months later, the property market has experienced a sudden reversal, resulting is in serious negative equity, with the bank refusing to release funds to enable her to complete her film score.

Questions:

- What are the ethical issues involved in this case?
- What are the competing values?
- How would you define duty in this case?
- What is the Natasha's duty?

THE IRONIC SENSE OF RESPONSIBILITY

The British psychologist Dr Meredith Belbin developed the Belbin team roles assessment to help assess people's strengths and weaknesses in teamwork. The test can be seen as a practical project management tool that provides a coherent system to explain individual behaviour and its influence on the success of project teams. The associated patterns are called team roles and the test classifies nine roles of individual behaviour in working teams.

We, the authors of this book, have applied the Belbin model in our work with student groups on both undergraduate and graduate courses at the University of Iceland for many years. Looking back over the notes we have taken based on our experience with students, it is the role of the Implementer (IMP) that our students seem most often to be identified with.

The role of the implementer is characterised as a disciplined reliable role, but conservative in habits. The strength of the implementer is that he or she has a capacity for taking practical steps and moves easily into action. The weakness of implementers is, however, that they are somewhat inflexible and can be slow to respond to new possibilities and challenges. This is interesting when discussing duty and its role in project management. The implementer is the dedicated organisation man or woman who is ready and willing to get things done and deliver results, seeing that as the main responsibility. Once on the move, he or she might not want to be disturbed or have their mission made more complicated by ethical constraints. This mentality comes in very handy when a project owner needs results, as the project leader sees it as his or her primary duty to accomplish and meet the project owner's needs. The irony is, however, that the implementer might still miss out on some essential things. They might be so eager to do things according to their sense of professional responsibility and excitement that they might lose sight of the wider picture. What comes to mind is the image of someone deeply concentrating on sawing the leg off the wooden chair they are sitting on.

In the light of the differences in management approach as highlighted in the Belbin assessment the project leader's duty could be mirrored in the success factor that is the project leader's leadership style. Turner and Müller (2005) undertook a literature review on this topic for the Project Management Institute (PMI) and found that the literature before 2005 did not mention leadership style too often or see leadership competence as a prominent project success factor.

THE IRON LAW OF DUTY

What is the ethical duty of the project leader and project team members? Who decides their duty? The implementer definitely has the capacity to execute defined plans but the natural questions are: who made this plan? Who defined the objectives? Who will assess the final success? Is it the board of the company, the government, the project owner or the project leader as an individual?

In the last two chapters, we explored outcome-oriented ethics, namely virtue ethics and utility ethics, while here we are looking at an ethical theory that strongly cautions against relying on any ethical justification solely grounded on outcome. Duty ethics warns against virtue ethics, claiming that justification for action cannot be grounded on the fact that it is good or bad for the doer. It also warns against applying utilitarian notions by saying that justification for a project cannot be based solely on outcome in terms of increasing/reducing the utility (happiness) for the many over the few. Instead of looking towards the outcome, this ethical method looks at the principles that should be honoured no matter what. Instead of being outcome-oriented ethics, it is process-oriented.

Process-oriented ethics focuses on moral obligations and moral principles, the rightness or wrongness of intentions or motives behind actions, such as respect for rights, duties, or principles. Following on from this, and considered, separately is the rightness or wrongness of the consequences of those actions (Olson, 1967). Process-oriented ethics maintains that the process used to decide upon an action/ decision predicts its rightfulness or integrity.

The field of duty ethics was strongly influenced by the writings of the German philosopher Immanuel Kant (1724–1804) and is usually referred to as deontological ethics. Deontology is the study of duty and responsibility. In Kant's view, the sole feature that gives an action a moral worth is not the outcome that is achieved by the action, but rather the motive that is behind it. The categorical imperative is Kant's famous statement of this duty, which, restated for our purpose, could be: take decisions on projects according to a maxim that you would like to establish as a universal law.

The strength of duty ethics is that it views sound morality as primarily concerned with duties and principles that require moral agents to behave in specific ways, regardless of the consequences. As such, the claims of these duties and principles may trump those of the greater good or the good of the majority (Baggini and Fosl, 2007).

Duty ethics would claim that good reason and sober rationality should be required in all projects initiated by humans, who are by definition rational beings. This is a necessary demand unless they have serious cognitive defects. From this viewpoint, projects based on rational choice cannot be based only on our personal desires, or the desires of the project owner or project stakeholders. They must, rather, be grounded on a *universal law* so they possess moral worth, and hence be justified only when we, by pursuing them, are doing our duty for duty's sake. This might sound rather complicated but, in fact, it is simple. When we do something, we must be willing to accept the fact that similar actions can also be taken, under the same conditions as we are under, by others at all times. It means that the present action now defines the right actions universally. It will become a universal principle for all, playing a similar role under similar conditions. Let us give an example. Should we allow ourselves to eat a burger with a large glass of Heineken in the classroom in front of our students in a session on project ethics? If we do it, or if we do not do it, we are defining that all university professors at all times can, under similar circumstances, do the same.

But does moral conscience based on duty insist that there is no moral worth in a project or action done for any motive other than duty? Is there no moral worth in actions based on virtue and utility, and, as we will discuss in next chapter, in protecting the rights of others? Let us take an example. We would probably be less inclined to praise a manager who rescues an employee from dying of cold while building a power-plant station if we learn that he did it solely because he wanted to feel good about it afterwards – (as he would do under a vague understanding of virtue ethics) – or because he could gain a reward from the labour unions or the government so that everyone would feel happy about it (as would be the case if he carried out the action under a vague conception of utility ethics) or if he acted 'only' because he was complying with a requirement demanding that he respect the rights of the employees.

Duty ethics, then, disagrees with all moral theories that claim that we should pursue good projects because they are the paths to happiness. It also opposes all ideas that regard benevolent or sympathetic feelings as the basis of morality. Kant made his distinction very clear between what he called *hypothetical* and *categorical imperatives*. A project initiated by a desire for a profitable outcome alone would be a *hypothetical imperative*, meaning that it would be an imperative applying *only* if we desire the goal in question (such as success, profit, and reputation). Such an approach is the basis for most pursuits in project management and the basis for all their related success criteria. For example: 'Project leaders should be honest in order to satisfy the demands of the organisation'; or 'Project leaders should be kind to their workers in distress, if they sympathise with their sufferings' are imperatives that apply only to project leaders in so far as they wish to be thought well of. In sharp contrast to such approaches, Kant said that morality should be based on *categorical imperatives*, that is, that they must apply to all rational beings, regardless of our wants and feelings. If we were to nail this down pragmatically in applicable, practical normative principles, then it could be as follows:

- Make sure that your conduct as a project leader can become a universal law that could apply to all people who might be in the same situation.
- As regards project choice, only choose projects or actions in such a way as you would like all others to do if they had the same opportunity of doing so.

MINIMAL AND OPTIMAL RESPONSIBILITIES

All project leaders know that they cannot have it all. They will have to aim for a solution that is best, or at least good enough, taking everything related to the project into consideration in terms of effectiveness and efficiency. The Iron Triangle can be looked at as a demonstration of system equilibrium. If all emphasis is put on time, we will have to accept increased cost and compromised quality. If all effort is put into quality, it will lead to increased cost and extend the time for finalisation, and so on. A project leader managing his project on the basis of the Iron Triangle will try to optimise the project in terms of the expectations given by interested parties. In order to assess those expectations, he or she will probably try to establish a range of minimum and maximum expectations for each dimension of the triangle. Taking all their findings into consideration, the project leaders will then make their decisions and define their strategy in cooperation with the project owner or the project sponsor, who is their representative and back-up within the host organisation. But the Iron Triangle is, as we have seen in the previous chapters, flawed in many aspects, especially when considered the context of ethical theory.

From a duty ethics perspective, if the duty of the project leader is, first and foremost, to optimise in terms time, cost and quality, then she/he should do that and not dwell too long on the outcome of the project, programme or portfolio. This is to say that the decision-making of how to do the job should not be grounded on the consequences. This does not mean, however, that one does not need to think about the outcome, but it just means how the project leader goes about his job is what primarily matters in this case. The focus is, therefore, not what will come out of it but how it will be done.

In defining one's duties within the project, one will have to establish well what these duties are, taking into consideration that all the actual actions that will be performed within the project will define the principles of one's approach. Action is everything for duty ethics and it is only in actions that the universal ethical principle is defined. A professional approach would be to identify the relevant interested parties and gather information about their interests and influence, then make sure that the project is executed according to all relevant guidelines, laws and in good cooperation with those involved. On top of that, each individual within the team, the team as a whole, the organisation and the even government should consider the categorical imperative – that is, say, to act only in such a way as any project team member, any project team, any project organisation and any society should be working.

WHO IS TO DECIDE?

Who is to decide the universal law and guiding ethical principle to be followed 'no matter what'? The short answer to this question is that ideally, it is the individual as a rational being who has to do this demanding task. Ideally also, the team's actions define the universal principles for teams, the organisation's actions define the principle for organisations, and society's actions define the universal law for society. It is, however, slightly more complicated than this and duty ethics is very clear on the responsibility of the individual. It all boils down to the individual who has to decide, despite all threats, what his duty is. This should be even more obvious to modern project leaders living in the post-Nuremberg Trials era. The excuse 'I was told to do this' is a very vague excuse. How would we like to live in a world where the universal law becomes 'you should always do what you are told to do, no matter what'? The one who is ultimately responsible and carries the burden of duty is the individual project leader.

The universal laws or guidelines applied by a dutiful project leader will also be applicable in his/her next project. In duty ethics, the Iron Triangle is no more than a useful model and first approach when identifying the duties of a project leader, because there can be many essential aspects to be taken into consideration. These aspects need to be taken into account and considered in the larger context of the big equation that defines the universal law, and should, according to duty ethics, be used as a tool for decision-making and planning throughout the project life cycle.

The experienced leader of a mountaineering rescue team that goes to the high terrains to rescue a group of people in jeopardy will manage his/her team and execute his/her leadership according to guidelines and rules that she/he has defined long in advance and has been trained in applying in difficult situations. When faced with deciding who will be rescued first, he will apply his rational judgement, grounded on long experience and guidelines, developed and applied many times over. Using the analogy of the Iron Triangle in this case, time is crucial. There are also strict limits to the risk he is willing to take in terms of cost, such as the safety of his team members. Quality is also crucial as he wants to rescue as many as possible and minimise the casualties and injuries.

For comparison, a different kind of a rescue team can be exemplified. A project leader is hired for a limited period to rescue a company that is going bankrupt. One of the obvious actions that must be taken is to cut operating costs. This cannot be done without reducing the number of employees. Firing people is not a pleasant undertaking, but this is obviously a main duty for the project leader in this case. This project leader knows that all project leaders under the same circumstances would need to do the same, and have the duty to do so, given that there are no other options available. The Iron Triangle is not very useful here, or even appropriate, except as a tool for professional assessment of how far the necessary cuts must be taken. In this case, it is the duty of the project leader to proceed in a professional way, to execute his skills in human relations, to behave with dignity and respect to the people that need to leave, and to make sure that all procedures are followed and the rights of the relevant employees are maintained. His duty is to do things in such a way that his conduct can become a universal law for project leaders in similar roles and in similar situations.

Case 7 – Gerard and Electra

Gerard is a project leader in a French electric utility company. He is managing a major maintenance project 'Electra' with the electricity transmission lines that cover south-east France. Part of the project is an inspection phase that entails having technical experts climb every mast to check the condition of certain technical components located close to the contactors of the electricity lines. The proximity to the contactors poses a critical health and safety risk to the person assigned to carry out this inspection task. To minimise the risk it is possible the turn off the electricity grid in the surrounding area. The cost of a shut-down is very high and there is a risk of legal claims from industrial customers and local municipalities. The most cost effective way to deal with the situation is to do the inspection manually with well-trained personnel, possibly paying high bonuses for this type of work.

Questions:

- What are the ethical issues involved in this case?
- What are the competing values?
- How would you define duty in this case?
- What is Gerard's duty?
- What is the employee's duty?

ROLES AND FUNCTIONS

The role of a project leader may be different from one project to another. Typically, a general job description is issued, defining the responsibilities and expectations, the boundaries of authority, the scope of the project and the type of the project organisation. Generally, the Iron Triangle is used as a starting point for discussing the role of a project leader. He is supposed to deliver the project outcome at the right cost and at the right time. His obligation is thus very much tied to the project sponsor, the client, the owner or the organisations that have hired him. He has a specific role and function in the project as the agent of these forces. However, he also has a role and a function with regard to a number of other parties in the project environment. These roles become more important and above the hiring organisation, based on the context and circumstances. For example, the project leader also has a role to play as a professional (regardless of his professional background), as a human being, and as a husband, wife, father, mother or friend.

A practical way of looking at this spectrum of roles and functions is through an assessment of interests and interested parties in a project. In every project, we need to ask ourselves who the interested parties are. These may be parties that have a direct interest in the project outcome, parties that are of importance for the project to be carried out, parties that have indirect influence on the project, and other parties that the project might have a desired or undesired impact on. The viewpoints of a whole range of institutions, groups of people, individuals, organisations representing different kinds of interests, may need to be assessed and taken into consideration.

The role we play in each circumstance defines the nature of our duties. One has, for instance, very different duties towards a child than towards a project owner. As project leaders play many different roles in life, they need to define what could be called penultimate duties, which are the duties that each role imposes, in contrast to the ultimate duty, which is to use reason to define the duty in each of our roles. In other words, the duties associated with roles might change, but the obligation to carry out one's duty according to rational principles cannot be compromised.

FEAR OF AUTHORITY

In discussions with project leaders we have often come across the idea that ethical decision-making is rather the responsibility of the board or the CEO of the organisation that the project owner rather than the project leader. Many project leaders fear losing their associated income or status for not complying with the demands of the project owner, feeling that they could easily be replaced with someone willing to act unquestioningly. This fear often gets translated into the notion that complying with the needs of the project owner is the primary duty of the project leader.

It is easy to imagine a conflict of interest whereby a project leader feels that in a project a certain action should be taken or a certain decision made, but is afraid of doing so out of fear of the authority of some interested parties. An example might be a project where the project owner expects the project leader to act in a certain manner for the best interests of the owner, but this decision might be debatable according to rules, laws, regulations, or even go against some basic values or beliefs of the project leader. A good way to approach this dilemma is to discuss the problem in terms of the interested parties and the interests the project leader is expected to safeguard. Duty ethics would say that the responsibility of a project leader has to be seen in a much wider context than just towards the project owner. It is, for sure, a part of being a good professional to be loyal to the owner or client, but this loyalty cannot, for a rational being, be unconditional or boundless. Obligations and responsibilities towards the profession, the authorities, family, friends, associates and, last but not least, towards oneself are also part of the duty that needs to be fulfilled. After this, the position must be communicated carefully and clearly to demonstrate to all how this course of action will deliver benefit in the medium to long term, not just in the short term.

A project leader 'blowing the whistle' as a consequence of wanting to do the right thing rather than the wrong thing, standing up for just causes, and being true to himself and his profession in a wider context, will invariably be better in the long term, even though his short-term interests may be jeopardised. A thorough analysis of interested parties and risks in the beginning stages and through the project life cycle is a useful tool for the prudent project leader. Project leaders now operate in post-Enron times and this should make them even more aware of their duty to be advocates of professionalism, integrity, social justice and sustainability.

OBLIGATION AND SENSE OF DUTY

The project leader and her/his actions can have a great impact on himself or herself, the team, the organisation, on society and on nature. Her/his work can be relevant for a large number of people, their calculations and conclusions can be of the greatest importance, and any loss of professionalism can lead to loss and harm. A project leader cannot, hence, claim that she/he has no professional responsibility beyond complying with the demands of whoever hires him/her. Duty ultimately boils down to the individual, their choice or perceived lack of choice, their actions or lack of actions. When put into the perspective of duty ethics, which demands the use of reason from the project leader, moral soundness is the project leader's sole option as a rational agent.

We could, of course, simply look at the duty of a project leader from a general point of view, and say that the project professional's primary duty is towards the general public and society as a whole. Then the duties of the project leader would be associated with the rights of others. However, as alluded to earlier, this will likely bring conflict as society often has the characteristic of having sectional interests. As the old saying goes: 'One man's meat is another man's poison.' Large projects in unspoilt or underdeveloped areas are, on the one hand, invariably supported by local people interested in gaining employment or generating related business, but, on the other hand, opposed by other local people on the basis that they are unsustainable and that the way of life, landscape or environment will be irreversibly damaged. One would, in this context, speak of the rights of the public and their range of needs in defining our duties. Ideally, this should be done from a long-term viewpoint as inherent flaws in projects have a way of manifesting themselves over time. It is hoped that project leaders are guided by a sense of responsibility to have a better and more sustainable impact on themselves, their teams, their client organisations, the society they are working within, and on the natural environment that all humans ultimately depend on.

On a different note, project professionals have a duty, just like all other professionals, to maintain their professional knowledge, experience and expertise. This means the duty of renew ingtheir knowledge and acting professionally in all undertakings. Hence, in a professional context, project leaders need to acknowledge that they are setting the professional example for all other project leaders and practitioners. Therefore, they have a duty to work with integrity and honesty, and to be worthy of the trust that the professional community, clients and end-users and the public place in them. As a rational being with analytical ability, the project leader has a duty to be critical and not afraid to draw her/his own professional conclusions and make them openly known when necessary.

We know from the discipline of group dynamics that people in groups often show herd-like behaviour. This, and the so-called phenomenon of groupthink, where individuals submit to the group – either to gain favour and acceptance, due to fear, or due to other unconscious group dynamics – can take the project team in a totally wrong direction. In such a situation, individuals, or the team itself, can start to make bad decisions based solely on primal needs within the group in the form of a sense of belonging, satisfaction of greed, fear of authority, mistaken understanding of professional duty. The resulting decisions are not based on what would be deemed as decent ethical conduct or good project management practice.

Reinhold Niebuhr (1892–1971) one of the great ethicists of the twentieth century, wrote a book with an interesting title in this area. Called *Moral Man, Immoral Society* (first published in 1932), the title suggests the fact that, at all times, there is a need for individuals to think for themselves and to be aware of tendencies to get side-tracked in terms of duty and responsibility because everyone else is doing so. The project leader is a key player in many of the most important endeavours that modern societies undertake, and often in a rough environment where values, people's rights, cultural and natural treasures are all too easily neglected in the pursuit of monetary rewards.

In duty project ethics, it is the duty of a project leader to ask critical questions, explain what is at stake for all stakeholders, inform and guide the project owner, the team, the host organisation and society. To maintain professional integrity, he should be willing to stop unfortunate developments and avoid bad decision-making, even if a group of people leans and puts pressure on him towards making a decision that he finds questionable. The project leader must be willing to take a firm stand in discussions with his superiors, the steering group, or the sponsor and be able to articulate the reasons for this clearly, powerfully and persuasively. He must not allow himself to participate in decisions or actions which he finds immoral or against his basic judgement of right and wrong, even if under the pressure from superiors. In such a case, the project leader must, in very extreme circumstances be willing to leave his post and 'blow the whistle' to inform the stakeholders about what is at stake and what is being compromised. In the long term, this would probably be a better decision than to participate in something questionable or wrong – and should that not be regarded as the primary duty of the professional project leader?

Questions for reflection:

- Do you only make choices with regard to projects that you would like everyone else to choose if they were in your position and able to do so?
- What duties do you have towards yourself as a project leader?
- What duties do you have towards your team?
- What duties do you have towards your organisation?
- What duties do you have towards society?
- What duties do you have towards your client?
- What duties do you have towards your profession?
- Which comes first – your duty to your organisation, or your duty towards your client? (Explain)
- Which comes first – your duty towards your organisation or towards society?
- Can all your professional actions as a project leader be taken as universal examples for all project leaders?
- How would you articulate your ethical views to your stakeholders?

CHAPTER 5

PROCESS-ORIENTED PROJECT ETHICS: RIGHTS ETHICS

Relativity applies to physics, not ethics.

Albert Einstein (1879–1955)

> Fully informed and with a clear conscience, are you sure that the project process (everything that happens within the project) fully values/respects all the essential rights of key agents/stakeholders/interested parties?

PROJECT MANAGEMENT PRIVILEGES

Project, programme and portfolio management is a privilege. It is a privilege to be able, capable and enabled to realise your own aspirations – or the aspirations of a team, organisation, business or society – through the defining, planning, organising and implementing of exciting projects, programmes or portfolios. It can, therefore, be a rewarding experience to have the professional competence and the rights to see fascinating ideas turned into reality through project management accomplishments. It is, further, a privilege to be able to work as a professional in a professional setting and within a competent group of people. And, still further, it is a great opportunity to be encouraged by society to build enterprises with licensed legal statutes and rights. All such endeavours touch upon the notion of rights.

We asked professional project leaders in Iceland about their understanding of rights by having them to respond to the statement '*Many projects impact people's rights in a constraining way.*' The results were that 14 per cent strongly disagreed, 32 per cent disagreed, 24 per cent were neutral, 19 per cent agreed, 3 per cent strongly agreed, and 8 per cent said it did not apply.

Iceland might be a positive example in this regard – despite its infamous recent reputation in banking – as it is a relatively just society that is grounded on human rights, legal principles and procedures. In many other places, however, especially in the developing world, corruption, crime, lack of transparency and injustice are often encountered. All too frequently, project leaders are at the forefront of decision-making and actualisation attempts in such circumstances. Ethically, this is both a curse and a blessing for the project leader. It is a curse, as injustice is often tied in with the profit-making interest that the project leader is hired to protect and actualise. It is a blessing, as the project leader might be the right person at the right place to do something about it and bring about change and development.

The last ethical principle to be explored has to do with professional privileges and rights. In the past, rights ethics – or justice ethics – was mainly concerned with the principle of human rights and justice, but in recent decades its notions have expanded to include the animal kingdom and nature. This development illustrates what can be said to be the gradual expansion of the ethical realm from the middle and higher-class white males towards women, children, other ethnicities, other classes, animals and nature. The project ethics of rights, like duty-based project ethics, is not concerned with virtue or utility and, therefore, not based on, or concerned with, the outcome or consequences of actions, nor the outcome of our projects. It has a much stronger link with duty ethics since it is built on the notion that once we have identified the rights of others, then it becomes our duty to respect them.

In the Project Ethics Matrix (PEM), rights-based ethics is focused, just like utility ethics, on the rights of all – in other words of each person within society. Rights-based ethics looks, as duty ethics, to the consequences of actions to the outcome of a project, programme or portfolio for the justification of an action, but at the process and the principle that guide the decision-making. In the PEM the rights ethics is illustrated as is shown in Figure 5.1.

The diagram (Figure 5.1) illustrates how the decisive point of departure in decision-making, if the decision is grounded on rights, is the here and now, and not the future consequences of the action. It also illustrates how the moral agent needs to look to all other people on whom his conduct might impact and to see their rights as fundamentally equal. Unlike utility ethics, there is no cost-benefit analysis to be carried out in order to protect the rights of the many rather than the few. To do justice is to see the rights of all as equal, no matter the consequences for either the individual or the many. The just thing to do is what matters.

Figure 5.1   Rights-based ethics regards the rights of all as fundamentally equal

The justification for classifying rights ethics on the collective side of the PEM, rather than on the side of individual-based ethics, is that its foundation is the so-called *social contract theory*. This demands equal rights be given to all, focusing on the many rather than on the individual.

PROJECT RIGHTS

Rights can be defined as the social, legal or ethical principles of entitlement, or in terms of having the ability to act and think independently. It is the principle that enables someone to do something or refrain from doing something. In project management it can, for instance, be said to be the right to design a project, plan it, execute it and receive the just compensation for doing so. Rights are, therefore, *normative rules* about what is owed to someone/something, or what is allowed to happen according to specific principles that can be defined by law, social convention or ethical theory. The concept is the basis of what defines a civilised society and is, hence, of vital importance for project management as a professional discipline.

The word *right* derives from the proto-Germanic word '*rekth*' meaning 'right' or 'direct', and the proto Indo-European term *reg-* meaning 'to move in a straight line' or 'to straighten or direct.' Historically, it has been used in many different ways and in many different contexts, but in project management it could be used as the right to plan, implement, execute and finalise a project.

But how far do our individual rights extend? John Stuart Mill, whom we met in the chapter on utilitarianism (Chapter 3), said that our rights extend all the way to the nose of the next person; therefore, we can conclude the other has the right to have us respect their space, freedom, and so on. There are likewise diverse possible ways to categorise rights, such as:

- Who has rights?
- What are we entitled to?
- What are others entitled to?

In consideration of rights, the project leader might consider:

- Who is alleged to have the right?
- Who has the right to express what?
- Who has the right to pass judgement?
- Who has the rights of privacy and when?
- Who has the right to remain silent and when?
- Who has the right to own what property?
- Who has bodily rights?

- What rights do right-holders have, and why?

If we see rights as universal, we can claim that all our entitlements can be said to be derived from nature – or from a more Christian worldview, from God – and hence totally applicable to all. If there is such an entitlement, then it does not depend on law, ethical theory or the custom or customs of any society. Rights necessarily exist and cannot be taken away.

UNIVERSAL RIGHTS

Universal laws can be called *moral rights, natural laws, inalienable rights*, such as the right to live, the right to have a home, the right to express one's opinions, the right to earn a living, the right to receive basic education. Legal rights, which are often also called *civil rights*, in contrast, are based on customs and laws of a specific society, such as the right to vote, the right to drive a car, and the right to build a house. The 13th century theologian Thomas Aquinas claimed that all rights should be grounded on natural laws, and should only be supported by laws and legislation. The utilitarian legal expert Jeremy Bentham (whom we met in Chapter 3) claimed that *legal rights* were the essence of all rights and he denied the existence of naturally given rights. If there are such things as universal moral laws then they are, naturally, something that the project leader would have to respect. The same holds true for all legal rights given by the legislative authorities in each society.

The most common notion of rights in project management is probably in the form of what is often named *claim rights*. These state that a person, team, organisation or society has a right against someone else as the right-holder. If someone has such a status, then someone else is not allowed to act in certain ways, or interfere in any way, and the laws of a particular jurisdiction will be invoked if an infringement is recorded. Such claim rights are something that every project leader knows and recognises as his or her duty to protect and safeguard, especially the rights of the project owner.

But there are other rights too, such as the so-called *liberty rights* or *liberty privileges*, which are permissions for the agent to do something without any obligations of other parties to do or not do anything. A classic example, which has been much debated historically within the western ethical and political tradition, is the right to free speech. The notion of free speech does not mean that anyone has to help another person to carry out their speech, or to listen to their speech, or even to refrain from stopping them from speaking, even though other rights, such as the right to be free from assault, may severely limit what others can do to stop them.

It can be seen from this that *claim rights* and *liberty rights* are opposites: a person might have a liberty right that permits him or her to do something only if there is no other person who has a claim right forbidding them from doing so; if, however, someone has a claim right against someone else, then the other person's liberty is limited. For example, we can have the liberty right to actualise a project or decide whether or not to do so, since there is no obligation either to do so or to refrain from doing so. But we may have an obligation not to do certain things, such as invade other people's private property, to which their owners have a claim right. So our liberty right to do a project extends up to the point where another's *claim right* limits our freedom.

Questions for reflection:

- How do you understand the notion of universality?
- How do you understand the notion of moral laws?
- How do you understand the notion of natural laws?
- How do you understand the notion of inalienable laws?
- How do you understand the notion of civil laws?
- How do you understand the notion of legal rights?
- Who gives us the rights?
- What are claim rights?
- How do you come across claim rights in your role as a project leader?
- What are liberty rights?
- How do you understand the notion of liberty privileges?
- How does the notion of liberty privileges apply to you professionally?

It is also possible to speak of positive rights and negative rights. *Positive rights* are entitlements to something or to do something, such as to offer a specific service or treatment when sufficiently qualified, or give permission to do something or give the rights to have something done to us. An example of a positive right is the purported right to welfare services or the right to a police back-up in emergency situations. *Negative rights*, on the other hand, can allow for or require inaction. They are permission not to do things, or entitlements to be left alone. This might further be translated into *active rights* that encompass 'privileges' and 'powers', and *passive rights* that encompass 'claims' and 'immunities'.

Questions for reflection:

- How do you understand the notion of positive rights?
- How do you understand the notion of negative rights?
- How do you understand the notion of active rights?

Rights are usually possessed by individuals, in the sense that they are permissions and entitlements to do things, which others, such as persons, governments or authorities, cannot infringe. The Russian-American philosopher Ayan Rand (1905–1982) argued that only individuals have rights, a philosophy she called objectivism.

Individual rights are entitlements held by individuals regardless of the groups they belong to. However, there can also be group rights, where certain entitlements are given to a collection of individuals, which is collectively seen as having its own rights, in and of itself. In such a case, the group becomes an enlarged agent, having a distinct will and power of action, and can be thought of as having rights. For example, in most countries, people that have reached a certain age threshold are considered to have distinct rights as a group, be it in the form of state pensions, special consideration for transport, or medical costs. In this case, being the required age entitles one to claim these rights. Another example is where business corporations are given similar rights to those of an individual that allows them to do things, or not have to do things, on the basis of these rights. Furthermore, members of a labour union might have certain additional rights because they belong to the union, including rights to specific working conditions or wages.

Sometimes, there is tension between the rights of individuals operating within groups. For instance, individual members of a project team may wish to have a wage higher than the union-negotiated wage, but are prevented from asking for more; other individuals might react negatively to restrictive work practices that can be a feature where unionised labour is strongly established. The question then becomes: 'Who decides how a grouping is going to define and act upon their collective interests?' Clearly, this can be a source of tension. Therefore, democratic structures need to be put in place and political decisions need to be made. Distributing, maintaining and safeguarding the rights of citizens can be said to be the essence of government and political life. Often, the development of these socio-political institutions has formed a dialectical relationship with rights.

Project leaders have to deal with issues of rights when their project infringes on legal or moral precepts, or when rights conflict. Issues of concern might, for instance, have to do with labour rights, disability rights, reproductive rights, patient rights, prisoner rights, animal rights, and the rights of nature, to name but a few. With the increasing demand for transparency and monitoring in our information society, we could also add the right to informed consent, information and the right to privacy. Modern professional project leaders also need to consider the rights of groups that have been or are discriminated against or marginalised, such as women, children, youth, parents, the elderly, those who have non-heterosexual orientation, disabled, and so on.

Practically speaking, the issues involving the rights of minority groups can surface on all levels and in subtle ways, such as in jokes or disrespectful remarks in conversations, and a lack of respect for special needs. The professional project leader has a key role in defining and enforcing awareness and cultivation of respect for everyone's rights. Even though rights-based ethics does not base its vindication upon such a premise, maintaining respect for other people's rights can ensure long-term respect for the project leader.

In this regard, a guiding principle could be the principle of equality. This can be portrayed as either equality in participation, such as the opportunity to take part in decision-making processes, or as equality in outcome, where fairness is achieved when more people have a more equal amount of goods and services from the project's outcome or processes (Roemer, 2005). Rights can also be authoritarian, meaning that an agent of authority is granted more rights than others, or hierarchical, where there is a change of command and a person of higher authority is granted more rights, or is asked to function as a protector of the rights of his or her subordinates.

• How do you understand equality?

More modern managerial notions of rights might emphasise liberty, equality and a flat management structure, where everybody has a realistic chance of being listened to and providing their own input into the overall direction of an entity. The newest indication of project rights ethics is the emphasis on sustainability and the intrinsic rights of nature and natural phenomena. Projects can be political, and all political endeavours can play a role in defining and recognising the above rights, and developing compatible solutions, so that projects can succeed without being cancelled due to the objections of some.

In order to understand the development of rights ethics, it is important to refer to the works of Thomas Hobbes (1588–1679) and John Locke (1632–1704), who established the foundations for our modern understanding of the subject. Hobbes was an English philosopher and is mainly remembered today for his work on political philosophy. He presented his social contract theory or natural rights theory in his book *Leviathan* (Hobbes, 1651), in which he set out his doctrine of the foundation of state and civil society. The book demonstrates the necessity of a strong central authority to avoid the evils of civil war. It was no coincidence that the book was published after the bloody civil war in England had ended.

THE SOCIAL CONTRACT

Hobbes starts with a rather mechanistic notion of humans and their passions, as he speculates on what life would look like in what he called 'The state of nature', where there is no government. In such an environment, one could say that each individual has a right to grab everything in the world, inevitably leading to a 'war of all against all' (Latin: *bellum omnium contra omnes*). This would, thus, be the natural state of affairs if there is no political orchestration, as Hobbes illustrates in the following paragraph:

> *In such condition, there is no place for industry; because the fruit thereof is uncertain: and consequently no culture of the earth; no navigation, nor use of the commodities that may be imported by sea; no commodious building; no*

*instruments of moving, and removing, such things as require much force; no
knowledge of the face of the earth; no account of time; no arts; no letters; no
society; and which is worst of all, continual fear, and danger of violent death;
and the life of man, solitary, poor, nasty, brutish, and short.* (Hobbes, 1651)

In a natural state, people live under constant fear, and their lives are a constant
struggle in an attempt to make a reasonable living. In order to avoid this scenario,
people accede to a social contract and establish a civilised society. Civil society is
a society under a sovereign authority, to whom all individuals in that society give
up some rights for the sake of protection. Hobbes' ideas gave rise to the social
contract theory. Hobbes argued that it is human nature to love oneself best and to
act with self-interest, but if we are to develop as a society, with mutual benefits
for all, then we need to look beyond ourselves and to agree to work together. The
core of the social contract is the notion that 'morality is embedded in rules which
dictate how people should treat each other, rules that sensible people agree to obey
for mutual benefits, provided others obey them as well' (Rachels, 1997).

Around the same time, the English philosopher John Locke also presented his
ideas about the contract theory in his book, *Second Treatise of Government*
(1689). Locke is the founder of classical liberal politics and believed that morality
could be deployed scientifically through an exact analysis of the terms used in
moral discourse, clarification of moral statements and systematic moral decision-
making. According to Locke, humans do not have any innate moral ideas.
Consequently, the criterion of what constitutes an ethically sound action is only
based on our sense of well-being. Individual rights, and therefore the rights of
all human beings, are, according to Locke, determined and given by nature or by
God. They are comprehended by humans, who are both capable of being rational
and dependent upon each other. Moral norms and values are the expression of our
rights that are taken as a given, being rational and identified with both divine law
and natural law. Moral laws must have due sanctions (rewards and punishments),
which are imposed on the will in such a manner as to restrain us from acting in the
wrong way. It is, according to Locke, impossible to speak of free will with pleasure
as the sole foundation of morality, as there would be no liberty of choice between
two different goods; the greater good would impose itself upon the will. There
exists, however, a liberty in the *execution of our projects*, insofar as the will can
deliberate and operate, or not, after such a deliberation.

Locke believed that society was ascending from a natural 'state' towards a new
state of society through a *social contract*. In nature, we did not live only in wild
conditions, as rights were based on physical strength and brute force. Even at this
time, however, Locke argued, we were somewhat rational, having the notion of the
fundamental rights of life, such as liberty and property. To better guarantee such
rights we have entered, through means of a contract, into society, and, because it

serves our purpose, have conceded some of our natural rights to the sovereign, such as the power to defend ourselves.

Based on this, a project leader who fails in her/his obligation to defend the rights of all stakeholders is no longer justified in her/his leadership role and should be dismissed. The good increases pleasure and diminishes pain within us. But not all good projects are morally good: both morally good and morally evil projects can be based on our voluntary conformity too, or disagreement in our project undertaking with law and regulations, where either good or evil is pushed upon on us, from the will and power of the law-maker or the regulatory authority. To safeguard against evil laws, good law, according to Locke, rests on God's will, which Locke claimed to be the 'the true ground of morality.'

- Main principle: make sure to pursue projects respectful of the given rights of all stakeholders (widely defined).
- Project choice: only choose projects that can be pursued by taking full notice of the rights of all involved.
- Project execution: only execute projects in such a way that the project takes full notice of the rights of all involved.

Project professionals who are interested in some of the background to human rights might want to examine the following documents for a more detailed notion of rights: the Constitution of Medina (AD 622, Arabia), the Magna Carta (1215, England), the Henrician Articles (1573, Poland-Lithuania), the Bill of Rights (1689, England), the Claim of Right (1689, Scotland), the Declaration of the Rights of Man and of the Citizen (1789, France), the United States Bill of Rights (1789–91), the Universal Declaration of Human Rights (1948), the European Convention on Human Rights (1950), the International Covenant on Civil and Political Rights (1966), the International Covenant on Economic, Social and Cultural Rights (1966), the Canadian Charter of Rights and Freedoms (1982) and the Charter of Fundamental Rights of the European Union (2000).

CLAIM TO PROPERTY AND PROFIT

John Locke was an advocate of property rights. In his *Second Treatise of Civil Government* (1690) he states that every human being has property in his personhood and nobody beside the individual has a right to this, only himself. Extending this argument, he states that the labour of the individual is also the property of the individual, and this leads to the idea that property ownership derives from one's labour. Locke, however, was, despite his brilliance, stuck with the notion of rights in his times. Therefore, he granted more rights to those who had more property, claiming that people who only had their labour to sell should not be given the same political power as those who owned property. Civil and political rights should be in proportion to the property owned. The right to property and the right to life were, for Locke, absolute rights, and it was the duty of the state to secure these rights for individuals. Locke argued that safeguarding natural rights, such as the right to property, along with the separation of powers and other check and balances, would help to curtail political abuses by the state.

Locke's arguments had a major impact on both the French and American Revolution, as the entitlement to civil and political rights, such as the right to vote, was tied to the notion of property in both cases. On the American side, the debate appears in the arguments of Benjamin Franklin (1706–1790) and Thomas Jefferson (1743–1826), who both opposed universal voting rights only for those who owned a 'stake' in society. This put them on the opposite side of the debate to one of the American 'Founding Fathers', John Adams (1735–1826), who felt that allowing universal voting rights would eventually 'prostrate all ranks to one common level'. In addition, James Madison (1751–1836) argued that extending the right to vote to all could lead to the rights to property and justice being 'overruled by a majority without property'. Even though the original idea had been to establish the right to vote for all males, eventually the right to vote was extended to white men who owned a considerable personal estate and real estate. This might surprise the reader. Would not a modern notion of rights entail there was a lot at 'stake' for all people of society? Perhaps, but that was not the notion in former times; it might conceivably not even be so in practice in modern times. The notion of stake is, namely, at the interface of the delicate balance between the notion of stakeholders as people who own something that needs to be protected from others, and the stake of the common person whose well-being depends on a just society and the rights to claim a 'stake' in it.

In France, Article 7 of the Declaration of the Rights of Man and of the Citizen (1789) states that no one 'may be deprived of property rights unless a legally established public necessity' requires it and upon condition of a just and previous indemnity'. Article 3 and Article 6 declare that 'all citizens have the right to contribute personally or through their representatives' to the political system, and that 'all citizens being equal before [the law], are equally admissible to all public offices, positions and employment according to their capacity, and without other distinction than that of virtues and talents'.

In practice, however, the French Revolution did not extend political and civil rights to all, although the property qualification required for such rights was lower than that established by the American revolutionaries. The French revolutionary Abbé Sieyés (1748–1836) said that:

> All the inhabitants of a country should enjoy the right of a passive citizen ... but those alone who contribute to the public establishment are the true shareholders in the great social enterprise. They alone are the true active citizens, the true members of the association.

The Declaration regarded domestic servants, women, and those who did not pay taxes equal to three days of labour, to be 'passive citizens'. The rights given to those with 'stakes' points to an interest in encouraging business activities and accumulation of property. Maximilien Robespierre (1758–1794), however, believed that accumulation of wealth should to be restricted and that the right to property should not violate the rights of poorer citizens. Robespierre's views were eventually excluded from the French Constitution of 1793 and the property qualification for civil and political rights was maintained.

Most developed societies encourage business activities, and people in free societies are permitted to aim for profit. The message is this: do it, earn from it, make profit from it, be admired for it, but do not violate the rights of others in the process.

JUSTICE AND OPPORTUNITY

Being allowed to pursue one's goals and to hold onto a significant part of what we have gained gives us a great sense of freedom, it is rewarding to see what we have worked on and created in our lifetime. If the patenting process had not been conceived, for example, it is doubtful that we would have been able to experience a lot of the wonders and convenience of modern technology. Scientists, developers and engineers would not have been personally incentivised to work on solving problems or creating new designs since their work could easily have been stolen, with no gain to themselves after all the time and effort they had applied. On the other hand, there are many stories of genuinely brilliant researchers whose ideas were misappropriated by others using their knowledge of the patenting system to gain advantage. So it should be borne in mind that sometimes opportunities can mean opportunities to exploit the work of others.

Of modern relevance to the field of rights-based project ethics is the work of the American philosopher John Rawls. In his book *A Theory of Justice* (1971, 1975, 1999), Rawls tries to solve the problem of distributive justice, which, for our purpose, is the field of normative ethics that aims to guide the practitioner in decision-making that has to do with the allocation of both the benefits and the burdens of any activity. Rawls tries to create a concept that builds on the social contract theory. He calls this the theory of 'Justice as Fairness'. Included in the theory are Rawls's two principles of justice: *the liberty principle* and *the difference principle*.

In trying to translate Rawls' theory into normative project ethics, we could say that liberty and equality are two principles of justice that can guide the conduct of the project leader. The project leader is naturally faced with scarcity and has to advance through cooperation with others in, hopefully, just terms. Rawls belongs to the social contract tradition and offers a model of a fair choice situation that the project leader could use to base his decisions on. This model contains an artificial concept that he terms the *original position*, where everyone defines justice from behind a *veil of ignorance* which blinds them to all the facts about themselves that might cloud their notion of justice. In this position:

> No-one knows his place in society, his class position or social status, nor does anyone know his fortune in the distribution of natural assets and abilities, his intelligence, strength, and the like. I shall even assume that the parties do not know their conceptions of the good or their special psychological propensities. The principles of justice are chosen behind a veil of ignorance. (Rawls, 1971: 54)

Ignorance of these details about oneself inevitably leads, according to Rawls, to principles that are fair to all. If project leaders would not know how they will end up in society, they will not privilege anyone but develop a mutually accepted principle of justice. Rawls might claim that a project leader in the *original position* would adopt an optimal strategy, which maximises the prospects of those who are least well off:

> They are the principles that rational and free persons concerned to further their own interests would accept in an initial position of equality as defining the fundamentals of the terms of their association. (Rawls, p. 11)

The notion of initial position is *hypothetical* and *non-historical* in that the principles are what the project leader *would* agree to, not what they have necessarily agreed to in the past. Rawls, therefore, would persuade the project leader through a process-oriented argument where one *would* have to agree upon if in the hypothetical situation of the original position.

Based on this, a project leader in the original position would take on two decision-making principles which would govern the assignment of rights and duties, and regulate distribution of social and economic advantages and disadvantages. Due to their mutuality, the principles would permit inequalities in the distribution of goods if and only if those inequalities benefited those who are worst off within society. This principle would be a rational choice for the project leader in the original position because he would agree to the fundamental idea that each member of society has an equal claim on the goods of the society. The project leader, behind the veil of ignorance, would also agree that natural traits should not affect this claim. Rawls argues that the inevitable conclusion is that inequality is acceptable only if it is to the advantage of those who are worst off.

- The first principle of justice states that: 'Each person is to have an equal right to the most extensive scheme of equal *basic liberties* compatible with a similar scheme of liberties for others.' (Rawls, 1971: 53)

The basic liberties of citizens are the political liberty to vote and run for office, freedom of speech and assembly, liberty of conscience, freedom of personal property, and freedom from arbitrary arrest. However, Rawls says:

> ... *liberties not on the list, for example, the right to own certain kinds of property, for example the means of production, and freedom of contract, as understood by the doctrine of laissez-faire, are not basic; and so they are not protected by the priority of the first principle.* (Rawls, 1971: 54)

The first principle aims at protecting everyone's universal rights, and, as such, it cannot be violated. In other words, the first principle is, under most conditions, prior to the second principle. However, because various basic liberties may conflict, it may be necessary to trade them off against each other for the sake of obtaining the largest possible system of rights. There is thus some uncertainty as to exactly what is mandated by the principle, and it is possible that a plurality of sets of liberties satisfies its requirements.

- The second principle of justice states that social and economic inequalities are to be arranged so that: (a) they are to be of the greatest benefit to the least-advantaged members of society (*the difference principle*); (b) offices and positions must be open to everyone under conditions of *fair equality of opportunity* (Rawls, 1971: 303).

Rawls's claim in (a) refers to a list of what he calls primary goods. Primary goods are the things which a rational man wants, irrespective of what else he might want and are justified only to the extent that they improve the lot of those who are worst off under that distribution, in comparison with the previous, equal, distribution.

The claim that equality is not to be achieved by worsening the position of the least advantaged also means that inequalities can actually exist just as long as they benefit the least well off. Morally arbitrary factors should not determine one's life chances or opportunities; and the project leader does not morally deserve his inborn talents and is thus not entitled to all the benefits he could possibly receive from them. The reference to *fair equality of opportunity* requires not only that positions are distributed according to merit, but that all have the rights to a reasonable opportunity to acquire the skills needed for the position.

APPROPRIATE CONDUCT

The idea of 'doing the right thing and doing the right things right' is a well-known cliché in project management circles. It requires appropriate conduct in project management, it might point to a level of respect for ourselves and others and, in order to reflect on their approach in this regard, the professional project leader should ask themselves the following questions:

- Do you think everyone has essentially the same rights?
- Do you go about your project management so that everyone included is respected as having essentially the same rights?
- Do you understand your privileges to work as a project leader as a right that is given to you by society?
- Do you define and protect the rights of those individual who work in your project team?
- Do you define and protect the rights of all stakeholders?
- Do you define and protect the rights of the organisation you are working for?
- Do you define the rights and protect the rights of the society you are working in?
- Which comes first for you? The rights of the organisation you are working for or the rights of society?

This comes back to our discussion in Chapter 2 on virtue ethics and professionalism, and the question whether we, as professionals, are first and foremost in the service of project owners and immediate stakeholders, or whether we evaluate our actions from a wider profession-based and society-based perspective.

STAKEHOLDERS AND THE PROJECT CONTRACT

Let us now take a more concise look at how the project leader should deal with rights by asking ourselves:

- Who gives the project owner the rights to actualise, accomplish, flourish, gain and lose?
- Who has given the project leader the right to profit?

The short answer is: others. It is society that gives project leaders the right to perform and gain from their undertaking. In principle, however, this right is not unlimited, but is restricted to, mutually, respecting the rights of society in our endeavours. It would be a vague notion of social responsibility to allow project leaders to gain at the obvious expense of society. The notion of mutuality comes across in both regulations and laws set by the lawmakers who, in democratic society, are the representatives of the people within that society. In modern societies, individuals, teams and organisations are encouraged through, for instance tax benefits, to create businesses and to self-actualise through different kinds of projects to earn income and foster development. The message is clear: 'Bring it on ... but respect society in the process.' The fundamental questions in this case are:

- Who has rights?
- Does everyone have the same rights?
- What/who gives us rights?

In our survey, the following results were obtained with respect to questions about how Icelandic project leaders view the rights of others:

- 58 per cent agreed (or strongly agreed) that everyone has the same rights; 21 per cent disagreed (or strongly agreed).
- 67 per cent agreed (or strongly agreed) that they execute their projects with the idea that everyone has the same rights; 13 per cent disagreed (or strongly agreed).
- 73 per cent agreed (or strongly agreed) that it is the project team's right that they (as project leaders) protect the team's rights; 4 per cent disagreed.
- 64 per cent agreed (or strongly agreed) that it is the organisation's right that they (as project leaders) protect the organisation's rights; 4 per cent disagreed.
- 72 per cent agreed (or strongly agreed) that it is the customer's right that they (as project leaders) protect the customer's rights; 1 per cent disagreed.
- 62 per cent agreed (or strongly agreed) that it is the society's right that they (as project leaders) protect the society's rights; 4 per cent disagreed.
- 16 per cent agreed (or strongly agreed) that the organisation's rights come before the customer's rights; 45 per cent disagreed (or strongly agreed) and 39 per cent were neutral or said that this question didn't apply to them.
- 7 per cent agreed (or strongly agreed) that the organisation's rights come before the society's rights; 55 per cent disagreed (or strongly agreed); 38 per cent were neutral or said that this question didn't apply to them (Sigurðarson, 2009).

It is a traditional notion in management that the shareholders of a company are the basic stakeholders; they are the owners and it is the primary duty of the firm to increase their value. A traditional model assumes that a firm runs a process where inputs from investors, suppliers and employees are transformed into outputs and shipped to markets where customers buy them. This returns capital benefits to the firm and its owners. When this model is applied for the purpose of identifying stakeholders, four basic parties are observed: investors, employees, suppliers and customers. From a modern viewpoint, this is a rather limited perspective, as stakeholder theory argues that there are other interested parties who must be taken into account. This is the theory of organisational management and business ethics which addresses morals and values in managing an organisation (Phillips, 2003). Stakeholder theory is useful for understanding a broader scope of stakeholders. It integrates a resource-based view, as well as a market-based and a socio-political view of the organisation. On this basis, the specific stakeholders of a firm, and the conditions under which they should be treated as stakeholders, are identified. As an example it can be argued that a broad range of parties can fall under the definition of stakeholders. These can be political groups, trade unions, governmental institutions, prospective customers and society in general.

In the more defined context of projects and project stakeholders, it can easily be argued that all projects in modern and historic times have had the purpose of satisfying the requirements of key stakeholders in order to achieve a successful outcome. Project success or failure has a strong link to the perceptions of stakeholders of the project value, as well as the relationship between the stakeholders and the project team and the project leader. The key to understanding the objectives in projects, and forming successful relationships in projects, is the awareness that different stakeholders see the project through different lenses and they have different expectations of the project and its outcomes. Understanding the expectations of stakeholders is thus a critical issue to address during the initial stages and throughout the project. In this way, the expectations and perceptions of stakeholders can be influenced by a project leader and project team that is/are experienced and skilled in communication.

Case 8 – Satyak and MoreMast

A mobile phone company has recently completed a project that expanded its services into a new market. The company hired Satyak, a PMP-certified project leader, as external project leader to manage the installation of a number of mobile phone masts in a built-up area to meet desired performance standards. This project has the working title 'MoreMast'. A number of sites have been investigated initially and seen as ideal by the company, but the contractor, based on basis of experience, believes that the local residents at a number of these proposed sites would object strongly on the amount of cosmetic and radiation health concerns. In addition, they might organise themselves into an effective opposition.

Questions:

- What are the competing values in this case?
- What are the ethical issues at stake?
- How would you define rights in this case?
- What can Satyak do?

A detailed knowledge of stakeholders' needs and desires is central to project planning. This consists of identifying, categorising and defining actions regarding stakeholders. Identifying stakeholders includes finding persons or groups of persons or organisations that are likely to influence or be influenced by the project. They are then categorised according to the degree to which they are influenced by the project and how they may influence the project. Finally, this information is compiled into the project plan. The strategy for execution is thus based on an assessment of the stakeholders, which will be seen in the work breakdown structure, the organisational chart and communication processes that are put into action for the project.

We can now see that this way of approaching the concept of stakes and stakeholders is closely related to the concept of rights; stakeholder theory is concurrently closely linked to schools of ethical thinking in management. Instead of talking about stakes, it is possible to talk about rights. The rights that a project leader must take into consideration when planning and executing a project can be addressed from a broad perspective. From the perspective of a project-driven organisation such as an engineering consultancy, a few basic categories of individuals, groups and organisations can be identified. These are basic stakeholders who have rights of which the project leader needs to be aware. The client is typically in the forefront when discussing stakeholders and rights. If the client of an engineering consultancy has hired the consultancy to do engineering work, then the consultancy should have the skills and experience to complete the project. This is the right of the client. It is furthermore their right to get technically and professionally solid solutions that are financially feasible, to be informed about the project progress and to receive timely information about any obstacles and problems in the project. The project leader must avoid all conflicts of interest. If they see such conflicts, for instance a relationship with competitors, contractors or suppliers, they should notify the client in time at the very least.

The project management profession and, in this case, the engineering profession, also have rights. The image of the profession should be preserved by using professional methods and working according to good practices and standards. Colleagues and competitors also have the right to be shown dignity and courtesy. In addition, society has clear rights that are often above other rights in the context of projects. They are concerned with safety, health and well-being, law and regulations of the society, and are always put in first place.

Let us take an example. You are the project leader of a technical project to build a geothermal power plant close to a road with heavy traffic. Based on your experience and expert knowledge, it is your conclusion that the chosen solution does not satisfy normal safety requirements regarding traffic on the road. You are afraid that in certain weather conditions, damp from the power station may concentrate on the road, creating hazardous driving conditions. You contact the designer and express your concerns. He does not agree with you. What do you do? The first alternative is to respect the judgement and contribution of the designer and do nothing. The second alternative is to put the safety of the public in first place and direct your concerns to the organisation that hired the designer to see how or if the design addresses this issue.

SUSTAINABILITY AND THE RIGHTS OF NATURE

Then there is the question of the 'rights' of the natural environment where some large engineering projects can have profound effects, some of which are direct and others which are indirect. This can put a lot of responsibility on the project leader to be aware of, and preserve the rights of the environment. To a large extent, these rights are stipulated in law and regulations, and the professions of project leader and engineering consultant all relevant regulations to be followed. People may have different opinions regarding sustainability of engineering solutions. This is a factor that can be calculated and taken into account when comparing solutions. However, in the end, the final solution is chosen based on a number of variables.

An example might be a controversial construction project, for instance a new motorway that traverses an area of undisturbed forest in an area already under threat from other developments. The public has rights to participate in a discussion regarding decisions to go forward with such a project, the environment has rights (sometimes considered as our grandchildren's rights) that decisions are made responsibly and aspects of sustainability maintained. If a decision is taken to move forward with such a project, then other rights come into play. The public has, for instance, a right to be informed about progress and that aspects of public safety are maintained and every precaution taken to ensure that the risk of casualties or accidents is minimised. This means that there can be obvious conflicts between the viewpoints of different interested parties and the project leader may be in a position where he needs to take a stand between the rights and expectations of the client on the one hand and the general public on the other. In the case above, he needs to assess future scenarios accurately and make a good professional judgement based on his background and experience.

Questions for reflection:

- What does it mean that everyone has the same rights?
- What would it entail to execute all your projects based on the idea that everyone has the same rights?
- What does it mean to have accepted one's rights as a project leader from society?
- What are the rights of the project leader?
- What are the rights of the project team?

- What are the rights or the organisation?
- What are the rights of society?
- How can the project leader protect the rights of society?
- What are the rights of the customer?
- How can you protect the rights of the customer?
- What would it mean if the organisation's rights come before the customer's rights?

Case 9 – You and WindPikes

You are working on behalf of an engineering consultancy on the planning of a new hydropower plant called the 'WindPikes' project, doing environmental assessment. There is some discussion in society with concerns being put forward and interest groups fighting against this project. You are participating in one of these groups as you are by heart against this project due to its environmental impact. You are asked by your friends in the group to participate in the public discussion by writing an article, expressing your professional concerns. The first alternative is to be truthful and honest to the organisation that hired you to do the work. In this case, you could have said no to this project in the first place. A second alternative is to write the article regardless of your obligations towards your employer and client. A third alternative might be to resign from your duties in the project and participate in public discussion with the full force of your beliefs.

- What do you do?
- What are the competing values at stake?
- Are there other alternatives?
- What is loyalty in this situation?

CHAPTER 6

PROJECT EVALUATION AND (ETHICAL) RISKS

In the preceding chapters, we have covered substantial ground describing different ethical theories and how they relate to the decision-making process, culminating, in each case, in a series of self-reflective questions for the project, programme or portfolio manager. In this chapter, we discuss how the full range of this ethical knowledge can be brought to bear on projects in order to establish overall ethical risk, and how the different ethical theories described relate to each other in practical terms.

It must be recognised that the modern professional project leader operates across a number of very different sectors and may work on very different types of projects. Making decisions on grey-area issues, where conflicting values are frequently encountered, is not an easy task and can ultimately involve situations like having to drastically cut budgets, fire people, instigate or defend a legal action, defend a project in the face of strong local opposition, face down personal threats, engage in bitter arguments with fellow professionals, or, as a last resort, decide to resign. Invariably in large, controversial projects, fellow professionals and the general public will carry out ongoing scrutiny and post-mortems, so that one's actions and motives as a project leader will be analysed in detail. As mentioned earlier, this usually leads to the formation of a consensus opinion though not too infrequently, two consensus opinions can emerge on either side of a political divide. As in the case of Chen Xing and the 1975 Banqiao Dam Disaster, however, competent project leaders who act in a professional manner by adhering to a strong ethical code will eventually become highly respected for the actions they have taken. Once lost, reputations are difficult to recover and it can happen that today's ignored stakeholder turns out to be tomorrow's project owner.

In the following sections, we will discuss the nature of project risk and ethical risk factors, and how these may be identified and planned for using a methodological approach that incorporates the four different ethical theories of virtue, utility, duty and rights.

CONVENTIONAL RISK MANAGEMENT

Risk is a part of all projects, regardless of their type. Some projects are riskier than others as a consequence of their nature, the environment in which they are executed, or the technology they are based upon. Important risk factors in projects relate to both internal and external factors, and all actions in projects, project management, or project work include at least some element of risk. Risk management can be a very wide and complex field, and is most often, as a result, approached using a structured methodology – the standard practices that project leaders typically apply to their projects to ensure a successful outcome. Risk management is inherently a part of project management so that every project leader is also a risk manager.

To many, risk denotes the potential negative impact on something of value that could arise from decision-making in regard to future processes or events. It refers to the probability of loss or danger that, even though uncertain and relative in an individual instance, can form a level of certainty in the aggregation of instances, or when looked at from an ethical perspective or from a more universal perspective.

In project management, risk could be defined as the possibility of an event occurring that will have an impact on our achievement of project objectives measured in terms of likely impact and likelihood. Risk management is the attempt to identify risk, develop strategies to manage it and/or lessen its impact with available resources. Strategies could, include avoiding the risk, reducing its negative effects, and/or accepting its consequences.

An illustrative example of diffuse risk potential could be as follows. A construction project leader in a well-known construction company is overseeing the laying of difficult foundations for a large hotel complex, where they are currently two-thirds of the way through stabilising the foundations. While he has focused on the technical risks and is satisfied with regards to the risks involved, he knows that the rainy season will begin in a few months, potentially bringing disastrous consequences for the project and causing a lot of local damage if the current phase is not completed before the onset of the rains. In the meantime, however, the bank providing the overdraft and loan facility used to manage the project cash flow has become a victim of the global financial crisis and has discontinued all previous arrangements. The project leader finds out about this at a meeting with his bank relationship manager. Despite a more than 30-year successful relationship between the company and the bank, the project leader is stonewalled when he points out that if he is not able to pay his workers next month they will walk off site, leaving behind an unfinished and dangerous situation. While it can be argued that this problem has come about to some extent by poor management foresight, it is an unprecedented event in the history of the company, and the project leader now faces a series of dilemmas, some of an ethical nature, to try to resolve the looming problems.

HOLISTIC RISK MANAGEMENT

The term 'risk' is usually associated with adversity, as pointed out by Ward and Chapman (Ward and Chapman, 2003). Project risks are considered to be potential negative effects on project performance. Project risk management would thus seem to be about identifying and managing threats to project performance. This view of project risk management is restrictive, however, as it fails to consider the management of opportunities – potential positive effects on project performance.

Kerzner discusses project risks with reference to the project life cycle, pointing out how the total project risk is reduced and the amount at stake is increased when the project progresses (Kerzner, 2009). Kerzner points out typical risk events at each of the typical phases of the project life cycle. The BS6079 standard gives an overview of typical risk factors in projects and divides them into such categories as human factors, politics, environmental issues, financial factors, commercial, technical/operational and legal factors.

Project management bodies of knowledge define risk in a broader way. The PMBOK defines risk as 'an uncertain event or condition that, if it occurs, has a positive or negative effect on a project objective' (PMI, 2004). The APM definition of a risk is 'an uncertain event or set of circumstances that, should it occur, will have an effect on the achievement of the project's objectives' (APM, 2004). Ward and Chapman point out that in order to emphasise the desirability of a balanced approach, the term 'uncertainty management' is increasingly used in preference to 'risk' or 'opportunity' management (Ward and Chapman, 2003).

In general, the risk management process is represented as a sequence of actions where risk is identified, analysed, evaluated and treated. This is represented in the Project Risk Assessment and Management (PRAM) Guide and is shown in Figure 6.1 (APM, 2004).

The process covers five steps. The process is iterative within itself and the output from each step might require a previous phase to be repeated. The first step, 'Initiate', is the initial definition phase of the project, seeking a common understanding of the project to which the risk management process is to be applied and fitting the general risk management process to the specific requirements of the project. The second step, 'Identify', is where risk events relevant to the project are identified as comprehensively as possible. What follows in steps 3–5 are ways of dealing with the risks that have been identified.

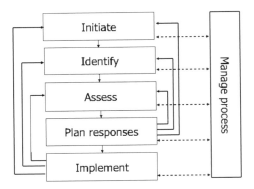

Figure 6.1   The PRAM guide
Source: *Project Risk Analysis and Management Guide*, Association for Project Management, United Kingdom, 2004.

Risk can arise from a variety of factors such as behaviour, environment, competition, technology, markets, organisations, financial factors, politics, law, and from variability associated with estimates, for example of the project time, cost and quality. Ward and Chapman (2003) divide the sources of project risk or uncertainty into four categories:

- Uncertainty about the basis of estimates resulting from, for example, who produced them, what form they are in, why certain assumptions were made, how and when they were compiled, and from what resources and experience bases.
- Uncertainty about design and logistics, owing to the fact that in the early phases of the project life cycle, the nature of the project deliverable and the process for producing it are fundamental uncertainties.
- Uncertainty about objectives and priorities, as some projects may be by their nature less defined at the beginning, and gain more certainty as they progress.
- Uncertainty about fundamental relationships between project parties, since the relationships between individuals and entities may remain harmonious or may turn acrimonious.

The third step of the PRAM process, 'Assess', is where the understanding of each identified risk event is increased to the point where decisions can be taken. Two dimensions must be taken into account: the probability of the risk occurring and the magnitude of impact on the project outcome, should the risk event happen. Both dimensions are an important part of the assessment as an event with a high probability of occurrence may have a low impact on the project outcome. Such an event reflects a low risk in the project. In the same way, an event with a low probability of occurrence and a high impact on the project outcome may still be considered a low risk factor for the project.

The BS6079 standard points out that in practice, obtaining adequate information for risk analysis is difficult (BS 6079-3: 2000). The standard lists some typical sources of information on risk probability and impact, including records and sources of historical data, reviews of research into project success and failure, experiments with prototypes, market testing and research, and application of different types of models. The standard furthermore points out that risk analysis can be conducted by both qualitative and quantitative methods, and the type of analysis should depend on the nature and quality of data available.

The fourth step of the PRAM process, 'Plan Responses', is where appropriate responses to individual risk events are determined. This will result in an iteration of the PRAM process, as the 'Plan Responses' step feeds back to the previous steps. This is because acting on risk responses will affect identified risk events and may result in emergent risk events as well as secondary risk events. In this step, it is necessary to be aware of interaction between actions; side effects that include consequences of an even more serious nature than the original risk factor. A simple example of this could be as follows: a delay in a project task is a typical risk factor, which may be met by the action of working overtime, with the possible benefit of compressing the schedule. However, the risk from this action may be more mistakes, higher costs and a longer schedule. A more descriptive review of such feedback loops is given by using system dynamics to describe the project as a system.

The fifth and final step of the PRAM process is 'Implement'. This is when appropriate and effective actions are taken, based on decisions made in the previous phase. The 'Manage Process' activity is a continuous activity throughout the process, ensuring that the risk management process remains effective. The process approach for each phase is reviewed. A common way of keeping track of the experience from the process – for ensuring that this and other projects will benefit from it – is to maintain a database of risk factors. This is discussed in the BS6079 standard (BSI, 2010). It recommends that this database should give an overview of all risk factors and document all decisions made in conjunction with the risk factors and their effects.

Questions for reflection:

- Who is responsible for identifying project risks?
- How can the project leader identify risk and opportunities?
- What might be left out in the conventional risk assessment?
- How do conversations about ethical issues take place in your projects?
- How do ethical issues come up in projects that you manage?

- Why should knowledge in ethical theory be part of the project leader's skill-set?
- How could you go about getting acquainted with project ethics and ethical theory?
- Whose responsibility is it to conduct an ethical risk assessment in project management practice? (Explain.)
- Is risk assessment always conducted in your projects?
- Why should ethical risk assessment be conducted in projects?

ETHICAL PROJECT RISK MANAGEMENT

Ethical risk assessment in project management focuses on risk that can be identified through ethical deliberation and the mirroring of project management objectives and processes in moral theory. The goal of ethical risk management is to reduce the probability of risk in general and to reduce the probability of moral risks of a pre-identified moral domain to the level that is acceptable to oneself and society in terms, as will be argued here, of virtue, utility, duty and rights. This is illustrated in Figure 6.2.

Ethical risk taking, therefore, can further be defined as working against our values, against the rights of others, and/or posing actions with undesired consequences, or by actualising ourselves through our projects in such ways that we do things we would not have done if we had thought of them carefully enough in an informed and ethically integrated way. Too often, it might be argued – and as can be seen, for instance, in the environmental threats we collectively face – in our undertakings we seem to take the somewhat privileged position of only exploring secondarily our projects from an ethical standpoint. Project management teaches that we should carefully weigh up projects before we initiate them, because encountering unanticipated problems and making critical alterations well into the project can add very significant costs to the original estimates.

In our consultancy work and when teaching project leaders, we have considered ethical factors in their projects and have asked project leaders whether they conduct ethical risk assessment. According to the survey, 91 per cent of the project leaders who were asked claim to have a basic knowledge in ethical theory; however, only about 31 per cent of them say that they conduct ethical risk assessment in their projects. We find the age distribution in the answers interesting. Of the project leaders who do conduct an ethical risk assessment, 4 per cent are younger than 30, 26 per cent are around 31–40, 48 per cent are around 41–50, and 22 per cent are around 51–60. According to this, project leaders between 41 and 60 are more likely to assess ethical risk in their projects than younger project leaders. Although only 31 per cent of the professional project leaders said they do conduct ethical risk assessment, 79 per cent said it should be a standard practice in project planning. Significantly, around 53 per cent say that they have identified ethical issues that have come up in their projects. About 49 per cent think they have the tools to evaluate ethical risks in projects properly, and 70 per cent say they would seek the opinion of a specialist in ethical theory if needed for their projects; 78 per cent say that the project leader is responsible for conducting an ethical risk assessment and 70 per cent think that the project owner is also responsible for it (Sigurðarson, 2009). If these results are representative of the project management profession in general, less than one-third of project leaders evaluate ethical risk factors or the ethical aspects of their projects before putting them into action. It can also be concluded from the answers that there is a need for an ethical risk assessment tool because only half of the project leaders think they have the proper tools to conduct such an assessment. This will be further discussed in the following sections.

In order to identify ethical risks in projects, we suggest that the project leader begins by looking at things from the perspective of those affected by decisions made. Within this, we identify five interrelated layers: individual, team, organisation, society and nature. This is illustrated below (Figure 6.2). Note that even though we use the term 'project' in the figure, this way of thinking applies to project, programmes and portfolios (PPP).

Having identified the potential ethical risk factors, we now need to apply our ethical knowledge to our decision-making process. Ethicists are well aware of the fact that morality, when looked at from a descriptive perspective, differs somewhat from cultural norms, values, and beliefs, and a considerable sensitivity to this fact is portrayed in the ICB Version 3. One aim, however, of *project ethics* is to offer

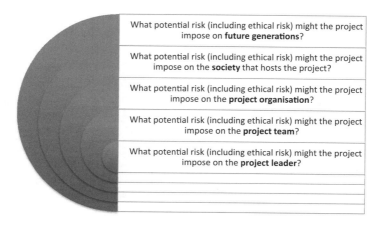

Figure 6.2   **Layers of risks (including ethical risk) and key ethical decision-making agents in project management**

principles and guidelines that enable us to deal with ethical decision-making by applying clarity in thinking, sound judgement and principled reasoning to reduce the risk of moral perils in projects, portfolios and programmes.

Moral values, which are at the heart of sound ethical decision-making, certainly reflect our understanding of self, our mission and our worldview, but ultimately our ethical conduct has to do with how we want to actualise ourselves. The relevance of project management is that it can help us to pursue our project management practices to good effect, and to develop ourselves in terms of who we ultimately want to be as individuals, teams, organisations and society – no more, no less – all interlinked. Consequently, we can view project ethics as a method to facilitate a maturation process and further leadership development within the discipline of project management.

As outlined in the preceding chapters, a holistic approach to ethics or morality can be viewed as revolving around the four basic concepts of *virtue*, *utility*, *duty* and *rights*. We have also seen that project ethics falls into two basic categories of *outcome-oriented ethics* and *process-oriented ethics*. Outcome-oriented ethics focuses on the product of one's actions or, in the case of projects, on the morality of its deliverable, and poses questions such as: 'Will it give good results?' Process-oriented ethics focuses on one's actions and poses questions such as: 'Is it in accordance with principles that should apply for all?'

What we propose is that before any project is initiated, the professional project leader should evaluate the undertaking from all of the above perspectives to decide whether or not to pursue it. And not only whether or not, to initiate the undertaking, but also if we do, how to go about it and how to communicate it to stakeholders. The four theories would hence be four different eyeglasses that should be used to critically examine the project.

THE NEW FIELD OF PROJECT ETHICS

The intended audience for this book is professionals who have dedicated themselves to work according to professional standards within the project management profession. We have illustrated how the field should no longer look at itself just as one career path among others, but rather as a proficient vocation that makes use of higher-order thinking to pursue its goals, guide its clients, and foster the disciplined, yet creative, development of the field into the future. We believe, therefore, that the project leaders of today and tomorrow must not only be specialised and trained in conventional project management theory, but ought also to have a solid grounding in ethical theory in order to be able to assess their projects thoroughly and make informed decisions. It is hoped that the examples given in this book of potential real-life ethical dilemmas have helped the reader understand their nature. As we have already argued, we believe that the basic prevailing toolbox for project leaders is somewhat lacking in overall scope; we feel that new elements are needed in order to help project leaders understand how they can include ethical analysis in their project preparation and execution. In our view, a qualified project leader is an expert in project management from a theoretical and practical point of view, and a vital part of his skill-set and toolbox should be practical tools for ethical analysis.

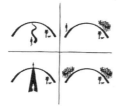

Virtue Ethics

Fully informed and with a clear conscience, are you sure that the project outcome will contribute to the long-term well-being of key agents/stakeholders/interested parties?

Utility Ethics

Fully informed and with a clear conscience, are you sure that the project outcome will contribute to the long-term collective (accumulated) well-being (more satisfaction/less pain) of the many, including, but not limited to, key agents/stakeholders/interested parties?

Duty Ethics

Fully informed and with a clear conscience, are you sure that the project process (everything that happens in the project) is managed in such a way that it could define a universal principle with regards to how projects should be managed?

Rights Ethics

Fully informed and with a clear conscience, are you sure that the project process (everything that happens within the project) fully values/respects all the essential rights of key agents/stakeholders/interested parties?

Figure 6.3 **The Project Ethics Matrix (PEM) and questions to identify potential risk (including ethical risk) in projects**

WIDE ROADS AND NARROW PATHS

To be a professional means to be capable of following a higher path of virtue in accordance with knowledge and wisdom. The Greek philosopher Socrates is reputed to have said that a life unexamined was not worth living, inferring that we should contemplate our life and all of our conduct critically with our reason. In this spirit, the aim of this book has been to show our readers the relevance of some classical ethical theory when added to the toolbox of project management in order to assess possible ethical risk in projects.

What we are advocating here is that future project leaders should, instead of rushing along the wide road that leads to apparent success, travel along the narrow path of project ethics that leads to sound and sustainable development. In our view, while travelling quickly on the wide road, it is more likely that we will demonstrate a disrespect for virtue, a narrowly defined understanding of duty, a short-term notion of utility, and a violation of rights. The narrow path, in contrast, though less busy, with steeper sides and a poorer surface of potholes and fallen rocks, will, by its challenging nature, test project professionals in terms of character and integrity, and is more likely to lead towards long-term happiness and success.

HEADING TOWARDS THE FUTURE ALONG THE CRITICAL PATH

As outlined previously, a structured approach is an integral part of professional project management, and we need this to guide us along the critical path of project success. Projects where a conflict of values is evident require great care in approach and willingness from project leaders on all levels, to be able to stand by any decisions made. In order to formulate this, we introduce a model that can, to a certain degree, be used to evaluate projects from an ethical perspective. It is based on the four principles of ethics that have been introduced in this book, and consists of five dimensions of interested bodies in any project, portfolio or programme: the *project leader, the project team, the organisation, society, and future generations*. These dimensions are combined with the basic factors of all projects: *resources*, *process* and *outcomes*. Together, these components of ethical principles, interest groups and project building blocks shape the ethical evaluation framework.

Each one of the interested bodies could also be said to be an ethical decision-making agent – even though future generations would have to be projected through a role-play exercise. If the interested bodies are represented by groups of people, then it is possible to split the group into four different subgroups, where each subgroup takes on the role of one of the four ethical principles explained in this book, engaging in what can be called a *community of ethical inquiry*. In the ethical inquiry, the ethical issues associated with the project are discussed and explored from four different angles, as each ethical principle is presented by someone within the group. The group then engages in a constructive debate to illuminate the ethical issues at stake. Such an approach enables the project leader and the team to become well aware of the ethical issues at stake. Such a dialogue could influence the project choice (which projects to pursue, which to avoid) and evaluate the ethical challenges that the project implementation might raise, as well as defining and preparing actions to meet these challenges.

THE KEY AGENTS

When the whole range of interest groups is found in modern project management and project success theory is considered, the conventional choice of interest groups – especially in the terms of stakeholders – may seem arbitrary. The groups chosen represent those that are the most directly affected by the project and will be affected if project is ethically unsound.

What we propose here, however, is that risk (including ethical risk) should be identified by representatives at five layers: the individual level, the team level, the organisation level, the social level and on the level of future generations. The decision-making agents should imagine themselves to be representatives of all these levels, and then think about the impact of their conduct on five levels: individual, team, organisation, society and future generations.

The *individual* is the project leader or any other individual within the project team; the *team* is the project team as such; the *organisation* is the association, foundation, business or institution that owns or hosts the project; and *society* is everyone else – hence society at large. The impact of the project interest groups differs with time: where the impact on the project team becomes apparent during the project's execution, the impact on the customer is more apparent after he or she has received the deliverable from the project. In this case, the project's deliverable will impact on the customer and possibly on later society; the potential risk of this key agent is identified under the term 'future generations'. All of the above should be considered against the background of the importance of nature and natural diversity, including the animal kingdom, vegetables, plants, water and bio-systems. This is touched on in the following questions:

- What is the ethical responsibility of the individual project leader? What risk is the project leader imposing on herself/ himself, the project team, the project organisation, the host society, and/or future generations?

- What is the ethical responsibility of the project team? What risk is the team imposing on the project leader, themselves, the organisation, the host society, and/or on future generations?
- What is the ethical responsibility of the organisation? What ethical risk is the organisation imposing on the individual, the team, itself, society, and/or the future generations?
- What is the ethical responsibility of the project organisation? What ethical risk is it imposing on itself, on the project leader, the project team, the host society, and/or on future generations?
- What ethical risk is the society that hosts the project imposing on itself, the project leader, the project team, the project organisation, and/or on future generations?

What is being proposed here is that when a new project is initiated, the project leader, the project team and the project owner need to evaluate whether the undertaking will have a negative impact on five different levels: the individual level, the team level, the organisational level, the social level and the environmental level. Both project processes and project outcomes could have an impact on any or everyone of these levels. The environment level is somewhat different to the other levels mentioned because, if the project causes damage to the environment, it might not have immediately discernible consequences or effects. Humans have only recently begun to realise that projects, consumption and corporate actualisation collectively are by and large impacting seriously on the animal kingdom and natural environment. The environment cannot rally and protect itself from further excessive impact with any direct action nor can it raise its voice or write newspaper articles. Rather it is society – or groups within it – this reacts when the environment is under fire from different organisations and must act as its voice. It has, therefore, to be people who represent the environment against the too intense intrusion of businesses. It is only when that happens that the environment gains a voice. Unless we are in the fictitious world of *Lord of the Rings*, where even the non-human trees can feel annoyed with the evils of the world, only people can raise their voices when confronted with the negative impact of projects, programmes or portfolios, or can cheer when faced with positive impact.

ESSENTIAL PROJECT ELEMENTS AND ETHICAL PRINCIPLES

The essential elements of most projects are project resources, project processes and project outcome. This sequence also represents the project life cycle in general and any of these three project elements can involve, or impose, a variety of ethical challenges upon different project bodies. In evaluating these elements ethically, the project leader should be able to spot possible ethical risks and, hopefully, manage them properly before a problem arises so that it does not compromise project processes nor impact the project success.

In the model, the ethical principles of virtue, utility, duty and rights are presented in the form of a list of questions. These principles are then used to ask questions about the project which the project leader, or anyone else interested in the project, can contemplate and answer accordingly. The goal is to encourage the project leader, project team, project organisation – and even the society that hosts the project (and future generations) – to reflect, identify and consider the ethical dilemmas that might be at stake. As it is not realistic to presume that project leaders in general have in-depth knowledge of ethical concepts, these concepts are boiled down and put forward in as simple and practical a form as possible. The focus is on project conduct both in terms of outcome and process.

We are now ready to introduce the project ethics evaluation scheme. In it all interested bodies – the individual, the team, the organisation, the society and future generations – are represented. The model should help identify scenarios where possible ethical issues might surface.

The PET (Project Ethics Tool) is made up of questions that are constructed according to the four ethical theories described in this book on the vertical side of the table, with the *interested bodies* on the horizontal side. The PET schema is meant to help project leaders identify ethical risks and enable them to reflect on and present these risks to the relevant parties, and make sound ethical decisions. But despite carrying out a PET, an independent third party is still required to answer the questions, so the third party's results can then also be presented with the schema and compared to the project leader's results.

The PET is a diagram that takes into consideration the five interested agents: (the project leaders (or any individual working on the project), the project team, the project organisation, the society within which the project is being actualised within, and future generations that the project might influence) in conjunction with the four ethical principles mentioned in this book (virtue ethics, utility ethics, duty ethics and rights ethics).

The list of questions within PET contains four main questions, based on the four ethical principles. The agent – project leader, project team, project organisation, host society, or someone analysing the project from the perspective of future generations – should answer the questions in the table thereby putting him/herself 'in the shoes' of each of the five key agents (stakeholders) mentioned. When all the questions in one question group have been answered for all the key agents, the project leader (assuming it is the project leader who completes the table) completes it by marking the results as follows:

1. If the answer is 'No', then it indicates that there might be an ethical risk involved.

PET (small) *		Categories of key agents (agents/stakeholders/interested parties)				
		Individual	Team	Organisation	Society	Future generations
		Identifies potential risks (including ethical risks) imposed on the project leader.	Identifies potential risks (including ethical risks) imposed on the project team.	Identifies potential risks (including ethical risks) imposed on the project organisation.	Identifies potential risks (including ethical risks) imposed on the society that hosts the project.	Identifies potential risks (including ethical risks) imposed on future generations.
VIRTUE ETHICS Risk identification based on project outcome for one(self).	Fully informed and with a clear conscience, are you sure that the project outcome will contribute to the long-term well-being of the following key agents?	Yes ( ) No ( ) Justify!	Yes ( ) No ( ) Justify!	Yes ( ) No ( ) Justify!	Yes ( ) No ( ) Justify!	Yes ( ) No ( ) Justify!
UTILITY ETHICS Risk identification based on project outcome for many.	Fully informed and with a clear conscience, are you sure that the project outcome will contribute to the long-term collective (accumulated) well-being (more satisfaction/less pain) of the many, including, but not limited to, the following agents?	Yes ( ) No ( ) Justify!	Yes ( ) No ( ) Justify!	Yes ( ) No ( ) Justify!	Yes ( ) No ( ) Justify!	Yes ( ) No ( ) Justify!
DUTY ETHICS Risk identification based on process in terms	Fully informed and with a clear conscience, are you sure that the project process (everything that is happens in the project) is managed in such a way that could define a universal principle with regard to how projects should be conducted by agents in the same role as the following key agents have for the current project?	Yes ( ) No ( ) Justify!	Yes ( ) No ( ) Justify!	Yes ( ) No ( ) Justify!	Yes ( ) No ( ) Justify!	Yes ( ) No ( ) Justify!
RIGHTS ETHICS Risk identification based (equal) process of the many.	Fully informed and with a clear conscience, are you sure that the project process (everything that is happens within the project) fully values/respects all the essential rights of the following key agents?	Yes ( ) No ( ) Justify!	Yes ( ) No ( ) Justify!	Yes ( ) No ( ) Justify!	Yes ( ) No ( ) Justify!	Yes ( ) No ( ) Justify!

*PET is the intellectual property of Nordica Consulting Group ehf.

Figure 6.4   The Project Ethics Tool (PET)

2. If the answer is 'YES', then it might indicate that there is no ethical risk at stake. We say it might indicate no ethical risk, but not necessarily, and hence the YES needs to be justified by reason.

The PET does not allow for the answer 'Not sure', as this might point to an ethical challenge and, therefore, the potential risk should be considered. It is possible that the project leader a bad feeling about some parts of his or her project beforehand. In such a case, answering this list of questions might confirm that feeling or possibly eliminate it. When all the questions have been answered, the PET is used to summarise the results. On a separate sheet of paper, the reasons and risks identified should be written down.

HOW TO USE THE PROJECT ETHICS TOOL (PET)

The project leader should keep the PET in mind at all stages of a project, i.e. when contracting, designing, planning, executing and handing the project over to the owner. Hopefully the exercise of filling out the PET will help the project leader to identify the ethical issues and risks that might be at stake. One should hope to accomplish this even though its use does not completely guarantee that the project might not contain unidentified ethical stakes or ethical risks that might surface.

Once the PET has been filled out, the project leader can use this information to inform the owner and sponsor, as well as other interested parties, and, if needed, to re-evaluate the project scope, plan and outcome in order to minimise the possible negative ethical impact on and of the project. If filling out the PET deems the project to be ethically sound, then the project leader, in dialogue with the project owner and project sponsor, might choose to continue with the proposed plans better aware of the possible ethical risks, or absence thereof.

Simple instructions for using the framework are as follows: (1) the scope and the plan for the project must be well advanced, if not completely ready, before it is mirrored in the PET. This is important so that new resources are not added or changes made to the project's processes and deliverables after being evaluated with the tool. If such changes are made, the results of the instrument are invalidated and the project needs to be re-evaluated with the tool; (2) the project leader – with the sponsor, the project team, key figures within the organisation, and even experts who might be capable of such an evaluation – goes through the list of the ethically oriented questions and answers them according to best *conscience*, with *all information at hand* and with a clear and *non-deceptive mind*; (3) an independent third party evaluate the project plan with the PET. This is especially important for high profile projects or projects in industries that might be very sensitive to ethical risks, lack of sound ethical decision-making, and failure. The independent third party is asked to use the PET to evaluate the project plan in the same way as the project leader, and the two results are compared. In critical projects, a trained and well-informed ethicist should be called in for such a consultation.

The PET is, in fact, an ethical quality control tool. By using it, the project leader confirms the ethical aspects of the project. Using the PET with ethical risk management is also possible, because the framework asks critical questions about the project, and the answers to those questions can be used as an input into risk assessment methods. In risk management, risks are assessed and pre-emptive actions planned in order to minimise potential risks. Risk implies that something 'might' happen, but issue implies that something 'is' and needs to be corrected. The greatest value in using this framework is the introspection that the project leader has to undertake in order to answer the questions truthfully. The questions require the project leader to evaluate different project parts from five different perspectives: the perspective of the project leader, the project team, the project organisation, the society that hosts the project and future generations.

The hope is that the PET can assist project leaders in better preparing their projects and make it possible for them to catch potential ethical issues that can impact on their own and their project's success. The research and its results as a whole might be an input into the continuous development of project management, both in terms of traditional success criteria and also ethics in project management.

TWO CASES FOR YOU TO TRY OUT THE PROJECT ETHICS TOOL (PET)

Case 10 – The ContraSave Accounts: New Type of European Savings Account

Number One Bank is an old and traditional bank in Controversia, a small European island in the Mediterranean Sea. The island is an independent democracy with a population of 500,000. It is an established democracy and the nation is proud and happy to be independent, not part of the European Union, though a full member of the European Economic Area. Controversia's main export has been fish products; the nation has an effective fishing fleet, it has a very powerful product development culture, and many companies are leaders in developing fish products and marketing them for the European mass market. Recently, tourism has become important for exports.

Number One Bank is historically a national bank, but was privatised in the 1990s, when a right-wing government was backed by a parliamentary majority for

12 years. The government carried out some important structural changes within the economy and national institutions. The Number One Bank has always been by far the largest bank in Controversia, but its size has grown drastically after privatisation and now the total annual turnover of the bank is three times the size of the national budget. This has had many consequences, including massive construction projects to build private flats and office buildings in Controversia, with the results that there is enormous demand for space. This has, of course, led to some concern within the bank, within the Controversia government, and not least among the lenders to Controversia state. International credit rating research organisations have maintained strong credit ratings for Controversia, and the government does not want to send out any signals about its concern. On official occasions, the prime minister and the finance minister speak optimistically about the status of the Number One Bank, the economy of Controversia and the future. They dismiss any critical questions as negative talk, based on lack of knowledge and understanding of the Controversia economy. The Number One Bank management has received clear signals from its lenders that a stop will be put on further lending to the bank in the near future.

Faced with this challenge, the bank's management is evaluating a revolutionary project to improve the situation. To reduce the dependency of the bank on its lenders, the bank is planning to enter the European life insurance market with a new type of savings account – ContraSave. ContraSave is to be based on a new and innovative IT system, allowing customers fast and easy access to their ContraSave account through a user-friendly interface on a web page, without ever having to visit the Number One Bank in person. Marketing will be designed and executed by a state-of-the-art PR consulting company. ContraSave will offer an interest rate that is very competitive in Europe, which is possible partly through a more streamlined process and direct transfer between the bank and the customer, thus avoiding the usual intermediate European banks. The management is confident that this will lead to a new inflow of fresh money to the bank. Potential customers are to be convinced that investments in their ContraSave accounts are completely safe, backed up by the Controversia state. The bank's management is comparing two basic alternatives: either to run the ContraSave accounts as part of the parent company in Controversia, or to run it through subsidiaries that could be established in any European country, where it will be supervised by the country's relevant authorities, though still under full ownership and for the sole interest of the Number One Bank.

Case 11 – Power Cable between Libertia and Europe

The concept of a submarine power cable between Libertia, an island in the Atlantic Ocean rich in renewable energy resources, and Europe has been studied many times during the past decades. The possibility of Libertia exporting its electricity to the European power markets has been considered to be an interesting option. The aim is to better utilise of the power plants and to get access to a larger market, to sell power when usage peaks on high prices. Last but not least it is considered necessary for Libertia to diversify its production, as 80 per cent of electricity produced in Libertia is presently sold to energy-intensive industries, mostly aluminium smelters. The National Power Company has thus set an objective to sell up to 10 per cent of its production as primary energy to Europe. The government in Libertia aware of, for instance, increased power prices in Europe, and increased demand for green energy, such as the Libertian energy, which originates from hydropower and geothermal power stations. Finally but not least, there have been considerable technical developments. These make a submarine cable technically possible and substantially reduce the investment costs. The cable would be 2,000 kilometres long, extending between Libertia and north Norway. It would carry 1,000 MW; the project execution would be 5 years, after a 5–9 year preparation period; and the cost is estimated at €3 billion. 6,500 GWh of energy would be sold annually and the lifetime of the cable is estimated at 30 years.

This is considered a technically possible and feasible project, and it could probably be financed. It is, however, a huge project on an international scale, by far the longest submarine cable ever built. Extensive studies are required on technical, operational and financial issues, as well as on the risk for the Libertian nation. A submarine cable to Europe would have consequences for many parties. Energy costs for the public in Libertia, as well as for industry in Libertia, would increase. The power companies would benefit enormously, utilisation of the resources would be easier and more efficient, and Libertia's export income would increase. It would be possible to balance higher energy costs to the public against lower taxes. This would nevertheless be a huge investment and a high risk for the Libertian nation. In particular, the feasibility of the energy-intensive industry in Libertia might be at risk if energy prices in Libertia were increased as a consequence of the cable.

CONCLUSIONS

We have now come to the end of this introduction to the field of project ethics. In the preceding chapters we have seen how, on a very practical level, the four ethical principles of virtue, utility, duty and rights, all grounded on classical ethical theory within the western intellectual tradition, can be used in project management. They enable the project leader, the team, the organisation, and even the decision-making authorities within society to filter out possible risk factors within, systematically projects.

IPMA, with its *ICB eye of competence*, has taken a big step towards the future by acknowledging the psychological and behavioural aspects of project management, along with contextual and technical competences. We will end by quoting John Stuart Mill. He once said that it is 'better to be Socrates dissatisfied than a fool satisfied', implying that pleasure comes from using higher-order thinking in our lives, even though the fool would be of a different opinion, because he or she has not experienced the kind of pleasure brought by intellectual integrity.

This book has focused both on processes and successes in project management in terms of project ethics. Our survey of the Icelandic IPMA-certified project leaders brought to light some interesting facts. Project leaders generally define project success criteria according to tradition – principally in terms of time, cost and quality – but with less emphasis on customer satisfaction. Less than half of the project leaders consulted doing the research conducted that their projects finished within time limits, within budget and met other project goals; more than half say that their project plans changed during project execution. About half the project leaders think that their projects have increased their organisation's success, though many project leaders do not think that their projects have business success objectives, or contribute to the organisational success. The majority think that, in most cases, their projects are successful in spite of poor results on the defined success criteria, which means that although time, cost and quality criteria fail and less than half try to measure the customer's satisfaction, the projects succeed. So, although one or many of the criteria fail, the project is a success according to the project leaders. It can be speculated that the criteria are defined in the preparation phase, but then the projects undergo alterations that the managers have to control.

For project success, it can thus be concluded that project leaders define project goals and criteria for their projects, but the results, according to the criteria, are failures in more than half the cases. The project leader's frequently deviate from the initial project planning, which means that the initially defined criteria come under pressure. Regardless of this, the projects are, in most cases, successful and make a positive impression on the customer, project team and organisation. When asked, the project leaders say that they have sound knowledge of ethical theory and around half state that they have the necessary tools to evaluate ethical risks in their projects. Only one-third conduct an ethical risk assessment, and the majority of that group are more experienced project leaders. The majority of the group concur that ethical risk assessment should be a standard practice when planning a project. They also say that they would seek the opinion of a specialist in ethics if needed for their projects. According to the results from the literature reviewed in this research, there is no good way or good tool for project leaders to measure ethical aspects of their projects. The fact that one-third of all project leaders actually perform an ethical risk assessment and that the group doing the assessment is composed mostly of experienced project leaders allows us to assume that learning from experience is the key through failures, project leaders learn to evaluate all aspects of their projects, including the ethical ones. In conclusion, the need for a tool to assist project leaders in evaluating the ethical aspects of their projects (and as a result, potential ethical issues and risks) seems to be apparent. The lack of tools and discussion about ethical perspectives in conjunction with projects in the project management literature also confirms this point.

This book has met the demand for a tool that builds on four key principles in western ethical theory, focusing on both process and outcome. What has been suggested is that these principles are used as a guiding light when the main elements of projects are evaluated at interest levels. By using this tool, the project leader must contemplate and find answers regarding his/her project introspectively. Project leaders may have a 'bad feeling' for a project they are managing, but may not be able to pinpoint it. The framework presented here can help in this respect – if the feeling is of authentic moral origin and guided by ethical intellectual ability – because the questions that are asked demand that the project is viewed from different ethical perspectives.

It is our hope that a deeper understanding of the importance and values of ethics will have the advantage of making future project leaders, project teams, project owners, and the associated societies feel even prouder about their actualisation through projects and their successes. We hope, too that awareness about ethical risks will help us bring about better project processes and better project outcomes. Finally, it may be that if people are happier in life might be more sustainable and abundant. In this sense, the field of project management is not a secondary discipline where project leaders are the voluntary slaves of sometimes amoral decision-making; it is a profession in the frontline of making this world a better place.

REFERENCES

Adams, C. (1998). 'A Kodak Moment: Advantix Names 1997 International Project of the Year', *PM Network*, 12(1), 21–27. Retrieved from www.pmi.org.

Anand, P. (1993). *Foundations of Rational Choice under Risk*. Oxford: Oxford University Press (reprinted 1995, 2002).

APM Publishing. (2000). *Body of Knowledge* (4th edn). High Wycombe, UK: Association for Project Management.

APM Publishing. (2004). *Project Risk Analysis and Management Guide* (2nd edn). High Wycombe, UK: Association for Project Management.

Aristotle. (1934). *Nicomachean Ethics*, dual text, trans. H. Rackham. Cambridge, MA: Harvard University Press.

Aristotle. (1999). *Nicomachean Ethics*, trans. Terence Irwin, 2nd edn. Indianapolis: Hackett Publishing.

Árnason, V. (1993). *Siðfræði lífs og dauða*. Reykjavik: Háskólaútgáfan.

Árnason, V. (1990). *Þættir úr sögu siðfræðinnar og stef úr samtímasiðfræði*. Háskóli Íslands, Reykjavik.

Atkinson, R. (1999). 'Project management: Cost, time and quality, two best guesses and a phenomenon, its time to accept other success criteria'. *International Journal of Project Management*, 17(6), 337–42.

Baccarini, D. (1999). 'The logical framework method for defining project success'. *Project Management Journal*, 30(4), 25–32.

Baggini, J. and Fosl, P.S. (2007). *The Ethics Toolkit*. Malden, MA: Blackwell Publishing.

Baker, B.N., Murphy, D.C. and Fisher, D. (1988). *Factors Affecting Project Success: Project Management Handbook* (2nd edn). New York: Van Nostrand Reinhold Co.

Bandler, J. (2003). 'Kodak's net falls 61%, hurt by switch to digital', *The Wall Street Journal*, 242(17).

Belassi, W. and Tukel, O.I. (1996). 'A new framework for determining critical/ success failure factors in projects'. *International Journal of Project Management*, 14(3), 141–52.

Bentham, J. (1789). *Introduction to the Principle of Morals and Legislation*. Oxford: Basil Blackwell, 1948.

Berger, J.O. (1985). *Statistical Decision Theory and Bayesian Analysis* (2nd edn). New York: Springer-Verlag, chapter 2.

Bernasconi, R. (1989). 'Heidegger's destruction of phronesis'. *Southern Journal of Philosophy* 28 Supplement, pp. 127–47.

BSI. (2010). British Standards Institute. BS6079-3:2010 Project management – Guide to the management of business related project risk.

Bryde, D.J. (2005). 'Methods for managing different perspectives of project success'. *British Journal of Management*, 16, 119–31.

Cicero. (2001). *On Obligations*, ed. P.G. Walsh. Oxford: Oxford University Press.

Cleland, D.I. and Ireland, L. (2002). *Project Management: Strategic Design and Implementation* (4th edn). New York: McGraw-Hill, vol. 1.

Cooke-Davies, T. (2002). 'The "real" success factors in projects'. *International Journal of Project Management*, 20, 185–90.

De Wit, A. (1988). 'Measurement of project success'. *International Journal of Project Management*, 6(3), 164–70.

Dvir, D, Raz, T. and Shenhar, A.J. (2003). 'An empirical analysis of the relationship between project planning and project success'. *International Journal of Project Management*, 21, 89–95.

Dvir, D. and Lechler, T. (2004). 'Plans are nothing, changing plans is everything: The impact of changes on project success'. *Research Policy*, 33, 1–15.

Dvir, D. (2005). 'Transferring projects to their final users: The effect of planning and preparations for commissioning on project success'. *International Journal of Project Management*, 23, 257–65.

Dvir, D. et al. (2006). 'Projects and project leaders: The relationship between project leaders' personality, project types and project success'. *Project Management Journal*, 37(5), 36–48.

Fishburn, P.C. (1970). *Utility Theory for Decision-Making*. Huntington, NY: Robert E. Krieger Publishing Co.

Flyvbjerg, B. (2001). *Making Social Science Matter: Why Social Inquiry Fails and How It Can Succeed Again*. Cambridge: Cambridge University Press.

Fortune, J. and White, D. (2006). 'Framing of project critical success factors by a systems model'. *International Journal of Project Management*, 24(1), 53–65.

Freeman, M. and Beale, P. (1992). 'Measuring Project Success'. *Project Management Journal*, 23(1), 8–18.

Geertz, C. (2001). 'Empowering Aristotle'. *Science*, 293, 461–9.

Gunnarsdóttir, A.H. and Ingason, H.Þ. (2007). *Afburðarárangur* (1st edn). Reykjavik: Háskólaútgáfan.

Harman, G. (1999). '*On Virtue Ethics*'. www.princeton.edu/~harman/Papers/Hursthouse.pdf. [accessed: 10 January 2012].

Hartmann, F.T. (2000). 'Don't park your brain outside: A practical guide to improving shareholder value with SMART project management' (1st edn). Upper Darby, PA: Project Management Institute.

Heidegger, M. (1997). *Plato's Sophist*. Bloomington: Indiana University Press.

Helgadóttir, H. (2007). 'The ethical dimension of project management'. *International Journal of Project Management*, 26, 743–8.

Henrie, M. and Souza-Poza, A. (2006). 'Project management: A cultural literary review'. *Project Management Journal*, 36(2), 5–14.

Hobbes, T. (1651). *Leviathan*, Chapter 13.

Hughes, G.J. (2001). *Aristotle on Ethics*. London: Routledge.

ICB Competence Baseline. (2006). Version 3, IPMA International Project Management Association.

Ingason, H.Þ. (2006). 'Árangur í verkefnum – Hvert er vægi áætlanagerðar', in *Yearbook of Engineering Association of Iceland (VFÍ/TFÍ)*, pp. 233–42.

Ingersoll, J.E. (1987). *Theory of Financial Decision-Making*. Totowa, NJ: Rowman and Littlefield, pp. 30–40.

Jugdev, K. and Müller, R. (2005). 'Retrospective look at our evolving understanding of project success'. *Project Management Journal*, Sylva, 36(4).

Kerzner, H. (1987). 'In search of excellence in project management'. *Journal of Systems Management*, 38(2), 30–40.

Kerzner, H. (2009). *Project Management: A Systems Approach to Planning, Scheduling and Controlling*, 10th edition. Wiley.

Kreps, D.M. (1988). *Notes on the Theory of Choice*. Boulder, CO: Westview Press.

Lester, D.H. (1998). 'Critical success factors for new product development'. *Research Technology Management*, 41(1), 36–40.

Lim, C.S. and Mohamed, M.Z. (1999). 'Criteria of project success: An exploratory re-examination'. *International Journal of Project Management*, 17(4), 243–8.

Liu, A.M.M. and Walker, A. (1998). 'Evaluation of project outcomes'. *Construction Management and Economics*, 16, 209–19.

Locke, J. (1690). *Two Treatises of Government*, ed. Peter Laslett. Cambridge: Cambridge University Press.

Loo, R. (2002). 'Tackling ethical dilemmas in project management using vignettes'. *International Journal of Project Management*, 20, 489–95.

MacIntyre, A. (1985). *After Virtue: A Study in Moral Theory*. London: Duckworth.

Marshall, A. (1920). *Principles of Economics: An Introductory Volume* (8th edn). London: Macmillan.

McNeill, W. (1999). *The Glance of the Eye: Heidegger, Aristotle, and the Ends of Theory*. Albany: State University of New York Press.

Meredith, J. and Mantel, S. (2003). *Project Management: A Managerial Approach* (5th edn). New York: John Wiley & Sons.

Mill, J.S. (1969). *Utilitarianism* [1863], in *J.S. Mill: Collected Works*, vol. 10, ed. J.M. Robson. Toronto: University of Toronto University Press.

Morris, P.W.G. and Hough, G.H. (1987). *The Anatomy of Major Projects: A Study of the Reality of Project Management*. New Jersey: John Wiley & Sons.

Munns, A.K. and Bjeirmi, B.F. (1996). 'The role of project management in achieving project success'. *International Journal of Project Management*, 14(2), 81–8.

Nash Jr., J.F. (1950). 'The bargaining problem'. *Econometrica*, 18(2), 155.

Nicoló, E. (1996). 'Fundamentals of the total ethical-risk analysis method (TERA method) with a study of crucial problems in managing distributed multimedia'. *International Journal of Project Management*, 14, 153–62.

Olson, R.G. (1967). 'Deontological Ethics', in *The Encyclopaedia of Philosophy*, ed. P. Edwards. London: Collier Macmillan, pp. 49–62.

Phillips, R. (2003). *Stakeholder Theory and Organizational Ethics*. Berrett-Koehler Publishers.

Pinto, J.K. and Covin, J.G. (1989). 'Critical factors in project implementation: a comparison of construction and R&D projects'. *Technovation*, 9(1), 49–62.

Pinto, J.K. and Slevin, D.P. (1987). 'Critical Factors in Successful Project Implementation'. *IEEE Transactions on Engineering Management*, 34(1), 22–8.

Pinto, J.K. and Slevin, D.P. (1988a). 'Project success: Definitions and measurement techniques', *Project Management Journal*, 19(1).

Pinto, J.K. and Slevin, D.P. (1988b). 'Critical success factors across the project life cycle'. *Project Management Journal*, 19(3).

Pinto, J.K. and Slevin, D.P. (1989). 'Critical success factors in R&D projects'. *Research Technology Management*, 32(1), 31–6.

Pinto, J.K. and Mantel, S.J. (1990). 'The Causes of Project Failure'. *IEEE Transactions on Engineering Management*, 37(4), 269–77.

Pinto, J.K. and Prescott, J.E. (1990). 'Planning and tactical factors in the project implementation process'. *Journal of Management Studies*, 27(3), 305–27.

Plous, S. (1993). *The Psychology of Judgement and Decision-Making*. New York: McGraw-Hill.

PMI. (2004). *A Guide to the Project Management Body of Knowledge* (PMBOK® Guide) (3rd edn). Newton Square, PA: PMI Publications.

PMI. (n.d.). Project Management Institute Code of Ethics and Professional Conduct. *www.pmi.org/PDF/AP_PMICodeofEthics.pdf*.

Procaccino, J.D. and Verner, J.M. (2006). 'Software project leaders and project success: An exploratory study'. *Journal of Systems and Software*, 79, 1541–51.

Rachels, J. (1997). *Stefnur og straumar í siðfræði*. Reykjavik: Siðfræðistofnun-Háskólaútgáfan.

Rawls, J. (1971). *A Theory of Justice*. Harvard University Press.

Raz, T., Shenhar, A.J. and Dvir, D. (2002). 'Risk management, project success and technological uncertainty'. *R&D Management*, 32(2).

Reidenbach, R.E. and Robin, D.P. (1990). 'Toward the development of a multidimensional scale for improving evaluations of business ethics'. *Journal of Business Ethics*, 9, 639–53.

Robinson, Joan. (1962). *Economic Philosophy*. London: Penguin Books.

Roemer, John E. (2005). 'Roemer on equality of opportunity'. *New Economist*. [accessed: 21 December 2009].

Rorty, A.O. (ed.) (1980). *Essays on Aristotle's Ethics*. Berkeley, CA: University of California Press.

Shenhar, A.J. and Wideman, R.M. (May 1996). 'Improving PM: Linking Success Criteria to Project Type'. Project Management Institute, Symposium, Southern Alberta Chapter, Calgary.

Shenhar, A.J., Levi, O. and Dvir, D. (1997). 'Mapping the dimensions of project success'. *Project Management Journal*, 28(2), 5–14.

Shenhar, A.J., Dvir, D., Levy, O., and Maltz, A. (2001). 'Project Success: A multidimensional strategic concept'. *Long Range Planning*, 34, 699–725.

Shenhar, A.J. et al. (2002). 'Refining the search for project success factors: A multivariate, typological approach'. *R & D Management*, 32(2), 111–27.

Shenhar, A.J. and Dvir, D. (2007). *Reinventing Project Management: The Diamond Approach to Successful Growth and Innovation*. Boston, MA: Harvard Business School Press.

Sigurðarson, S.F. (2009). 'Critical Success Factors in Project Management: An ethical perspective'. http://skemman.is/handle/1946/3020 [accessed: 9 June 2009].

Singer, P. (ed.) (1990). *A Companion to Ethics*. Oxford: Basil Blackwell.

Sorabji, R. (1973/74). 'Aristotle on the role of intellect in virtue'. *Proceedings of the Aristotelian Society* 74, 107–29.

Stackhouse, M.L. (1995) 'Introduction: Foundations and Purposes' in M.L. Stackhouse, D.P. McCann, S.J. Roels, P.N. Williams (eds) (1995). *On Moral Business: Classical and Contemporary Resources for Ethics in Economic Life*. Michigan: William B. Eerdmans Publishing Company.

Stanford Encyclopedia of Philosophy. 'Hobbes's Moral and Political Philosophy'. http://plato.stanford.edu/entries/hobbes-moral/. [accessed: 11 March 2009].

Themistocleous, G. and Wearne, S.H. (2000). 'Project management topic coverage in journals'. *International Journal of Project Management*, 18, 7–11.

Turner, J.R. (1999). *Handbook of Project-Based Management: Improving the Process for Achieving Strategic Objectives* (2nd edn). London: McGraw-Hill.

Turner, J.R. and Müller, R. (2005). 'The project leader's leadership style as a success factor on projects: A review'. *Project Management Journal*, 36(2), 49–61.

Ward, S. and Chapman, C. (2003). 'Transforming project risk management into project uncertainty management'. *International Journal of Project Management*, 21, 97–105.

Wateridge, J. (1995). 'IT projects: A basis for success'. *International Journal of Project Management*, 13(3), 169–72.

Wells, W.G. Jr. (1998). 'The changing nature of project management'. *Project Management Journal*, 29(1).

Wenell, T. (2000). *Wenell om project*. Uppsala, Sweden: Konsultförlage.

Westerveld, E. (2003). 'The Project Excellence Model®: Linking success criteria and critical success factors'. *International Journal of Project Management*, 21, 411–18.

Wiggins, D. (1975–76). 'Deliberation and practical reason'. *Proceedings of the Aristotelian Society* 76, 29–51.

INDEX

ADVANCES IN PROJECT MANAGEMENT

Advances in Project Management provides short, state of play, guides to the main aspects of the new emerging applications including: maturity models, agile projects, extreme projects, Six Sigma and projects, human factors and leadership in projects, project governance, value management, virtual teams and project benefits.

CURRENTLY PUBLISHED TITLES

Managing Project Uncertainty, David Cleden 978-0-566-08840-7

Managing Project Supply Chains, Ron Basu 978-1-4094-2515-1

Project-Oriented Leadership, Ralf Müller and J Rodney Turner 978-0-566-08923-7

Strategic Project Risk Appraisal and Management, Elaine Harris 978-0-566-08848-3

Spirituality and Project Management, Judi Neal and Alan Harpham 978-1-4094-0959-5

Sustainability in Project Management, Gilbert Silvius, Jasper van den Brink, Ron Schipper, Adri Köhler and Julia Planko 978-1-4094-3169-5

Second Order Project Management, Michael Cavanagh, 978-1-4094-1094-2

Tame, Messy and Wicked Risk Leadership, David Hancock 978-0-566-09242-8

REVIEWS OF THE SERIES

Managing Project Uncertainty, David Cleden

> *This is a must-read book for anyone involved in project management. The author's carefully crafted work meets all my "4Cs" review criteria. The book is clear, cogent, concise and complete...it is a brave author who essays to write about managing project uncertainty in a text extending to only 117 pages (soft-cover version). In my opinion, David Cleden succeeds brilliantly...For project managers this book, far from being a short-lived stress anodyne, will provide a confidence-boosting tonic. Project uncertainty? Bring it on, I say!*
>
> International Journal of Managing Projects in Business

> *Uncertainty is an inevitable aspect of most projects, but even the most proficient project manager struggles to successfully contain it. Many projects overrun and consume more funds than were originally budgeted, often leading to unplanned expense and outright programme failure. David examines how uncertainty occurs and provides management strategies that the user can put to immediate use on their own project work. He also provides a series of pre-emptive uncertainty and risk avoidance strategies that should be the cornerstone of any planning exercise for all personnel involved in project work.*
>
> *I have been delivering both large and small projects and programmes in the public and private sector since 1989. I wish this book had been available when I began my career in project work. I strongly commend this book to all project professionals.*
>
> Lee Hendricks, Sales & Marketing Director, SunGard Public Sector

> *The book under review is an excellent presentation of a comprehensive set of explorations about uncertainty (its recognition) in the context of projects. It does a good job of all along reinforcing the difference between risk (known unknowns) management and managing uncertainty (unknown unknowns - "bolt from the blue"). The author lucidly presents a variety of frameworks/ models so that the reader easily grasps the varied forms in which uncertainty presents itself in the context of projects.*
>
> VISION – The Journal of Business Perspective (India)

> *Cleden will leave you with a sound understanding about the traits, tendencies, timing and tenacity of uncertainty in projects. He is also adept at identifying certain methods that try to contain the uncertainty, and why some prove more successful than others. Those who expect risk management to be the be-all, end-all for uncertainty solutions will be in for a rude awakening.*
>
> Brad Egeland, Project Management Tips

Project-Oriented Leadership, Rodney Turner and Ralf Müller

> *Müller and Turner have compiled a terrific "ready-reckoner" that all project managers would benefit from reading and reflecting upon to challenge their performance. The authors have condensed considerable experience and research from a wide variety of professional disciplines, to provide a robust digest that highlights the significance of leadership capabilities for effective delivery of project outcomes. One of the big advantages of this book is the richness of the content and the natural flow of their argument throughout such a short book....Good advice, well explained and backed up with a body of evidence...I will be recommending the book to colleagues who are in project leader and manager roles and to students who are considering these as part of their development or career path.*

> Arthur Shelley, RMIT University, Melbourne, Australia, International Journal of Managing Projects in Business

> *In a remarkably succinct 89 pages, Müller and Turner review an astonishing depth of evidence, supported by their own (published) research which challenges many of the commonly held assumptions not only about project management, but about what makes for successful leaders.*

> *This book is clearly written more for the project-manager type personality than for the natural leader. Concision, evidence and analysis are the main characteristics of the writing style...it is massively authoritative, and so carefully written that a couple of hours spent in its 89 pages may pay huge dividends compared to the more expansive, easy reading style of other management books.*

> Mike Turner, Director of Communications for NHS Warwickshire

Strategic Project Risk Appraisal and Management, Elaine Harris

> *...Elaine Harris's volume is timely. In a world of books by "instant experts" it's pleasing to read something by someone who clearly knows their onions, and has a passion for the subject...In summary, this is a thorough and engaging book.*

> Chris Morgan, Head of Business Assurance for Select Plant Hire, Quality World

> *As soon as I met Elaine I realised that we both shared a passion to better understand the inherent risk in any project, be that capital investment, expansion capital or expansion of assets. What is seldom analysed are the components of knowledge necessary to make a good judgement, the impact of our own prejudices in relation to projects or for that matter the cultural elements within an organisation which impact upon the decision making process. Elaine created a system to break this down and give reasons and*

logic to both the process and the human interaction necessary to improve the chances of success. Adopting her recommendations will improve teamwork and outcomes for your company.

Edward Roderick Hon LLD, Former CEO Christian Salvesen Plc

Tame, Messy and Wicked Risk Leadership, David Hancock

This book takes project risk management firmly onto a higher and wider plane. We thought we knew what project risk management was and what it could do. David Hancock shows us a great deal more of both. David Hancock has probably read more about risk management than almost anybody else, he has almost certainly thought about it as much as anybody else and he has quite certainly learnt from doing it on very difficult projects as much as anybody else. His book draws fully on all three components. For a book which tackles a complex subject with breadth, insight and novelty - its remarkable that it is also a really good read. I could go on!

Dr Martin Barnes CBE FREng, President, The Association for Project Management

This compact and thought provoking description of risk management will be useful to anybody with responsibilities for projects, programmes or businesses. It hits the nail on the head in so many ways, for example by pointing out that risk management can easily drift into a check-list mindset, driven by the production of registers of numerous occurrences characterised by the Risk = Probablity x Consequence equation. David Hancock points out that real life is much more complicated, with the heart of the problem lying in people, so that real life resembles poker rather than roulette. He also points out that while the important thing is to solve the right problem, many real life issues cannot be readily described in a definitive statement of the problem. There are often interrelated individual problems with surrounding social issues and he describes these real life situations as 'Wicked Messes'. Unusual terminology, but definitely worth the read, as much for the overall problem description as for the recommended strategies for getting to grips with real life risk management. I have no hesitation in recommending this book.

Sir Robert Walmsley KCB FREng, Chairman of the Board of the Major Projects Association

In highlighting the complexity of many of today's problems and defining them as tame, messy or wicked, David Hancock brings a new perspective to the risk issues that we currently face. He challenges risk managers, and particularly those involved in project risk management, to take a much broader approach to the assessment of risk and consider the social, political and behavioural dimensions of each problem, as well as the scientific and engineering aspects with which they are most comfortable. In this way, risks will be viewed more holistically and managed more effectively than at present.

Dr Lynn T Drennan, Chief Executive, Alarm, the public risk management association

Sustainability in Project Management, Gilbert Silvius, Jasper van den Brink, Ron Schipper, Adri Köhler and Julia Planko

Sustainability in Project Management thinking and techniques is still in its relatively early days. By the end of this decade it will probably be universal, ubiquitous, fully integrated and expected. This book will be a most valuable guide on this journey for all those interested in the future of projects and how they are managed in a world in peril.

Tom Taylor dashdot and vice-President of APM

Project Managers are faced with lots of intersections. The intersection of projects and risk, projects and people, projects and constraints ... Sustainability in Projects and Project Management is a compelling, in-depth treatment of a most important intersection: the intersection of project management and sustainability. With detailed background building to practical checklists and a call to action, this book is a must-read for anyone interested in truly implementing sustainability, project manager or not.

Rich Maltzman, PMP, Co-Founder, EarthPM, LLC, and co-author of Green Project Management, Cleland Literature Award Winner of 2011

Great book! Based on a thorough review on existing relevant models and concepts the authors provide guidance for different stakeholders such as Project Managers and Project Office Managers to consider sustainability principles on projects. The book gets you started on sustainability in project context!

Martina Huemann, WU-Vienna University of Economics and Business, Vienna Austria

While sustainability and green business have been around a while, this book is truly a "call to action" to help the project manager, or for that matter, anyone, seize the day and understand sustainability from a project perspective. This book gives real and practical suggestions as to how to fill the sustainability/ project gap within your organization. I particularly liked the relationship between sustainability and "professionalism and ethics", a connection that needs to be kept in the forefront.

David Shirley, PMP, Co-Founder, EarthPM, LLC, and co-author of Green Project Management, Cleland Literature Award Winner of 2011

It is high time that quality corporate citizenship takes its place outside the corporate board room. This excellent work, which places the effort needed to secure sustainability for everything we do right where the rubber hits the road – our projects – has been long overdue. Thank you Gilbert, Jasper, Ron, Adri and Julia for doing just that! I salute you.

Jaycee Krüger, member of ISO/TC258 a technical committee for the creation of standards in Project, Program and Portfolio Management, and chair of SABS/TC258, the South African mirror committee of ISO/TC258

Sustainability is no passing fad. It is the moral obligation that we all face in ensuring the future of human generations to come. The need to show stewardship and act as sustainability change agents has never been greater. As project managers we are at the forefront of influencing the direction of our projects and our organisations. Sustainability in Project Management offers illuminating insights into the concept of sustainability and its application to project management. It is a must read for any modern project manager.

Dr Neveen Moussa, Project Manager, Adjunct Professor of Project Management and past president of the Australian Institute of Project Management

ABOUT THE EDITOR

Professor Darren Dalcher is founder and Director of the National Centre for Project Management, a Professor of Project Management at the University of Hertfordshire and Visiting Professor of Computer Science at the University of Iceland.

Following industrial and consultancy experience in managing IT projects, Professor Dalcher gained his PhD from King's College, University of London. In 1992, he founded and chaired of the Forensics Working Group of the IEEE Technical Committee on the Engineering of Computer-Based Systems, an international group of academic and industrial participants formed to share information and develop expertise in project and system failure and recovery.

He is active in numerous international committees, standards bodies, steering groups, and editorial boards. He is heavily involved in organising international conferences, and has delivered many international keynote addresses and tutorials. He has written over 150 refereed papers and book chapters on project management and software engineering. He is Editor-in-Chief of the *International Journal of Software Maintenance and Evolution*, and of the *Journal of Software: Evolution and Process*. He is the editor of a major new book series, Advances in Project Management, published by Gower Publishing which synthesises leading edge knowledge, skills, insights and reflections in project and programme management and of a new companion series, Fundamentals of Project Management, which provides the essential grounding in key areas of project management.

He has built a reputation as leader and innovator in the area of practice-based education and reflection in project management and has worked with many major industrial, commercial and charitable organisations and government bodies. In 2008 he was named by the Association for Project Management as one of the top 10 influential experts in project management and has also been voted *Project Magazine's* Academic of the Year for his contribution in "integrating and weaving academic work with practice". He has been chairman of the APM Project Management Conference since 2009, setting consecutive attendance records and bringing together the most influential speakers.

He received international recognition in 2009 with appointment as a member of the PMForum International Academic Advisory Council, which features leading academics from some of the world's top universities and academic institutions. The Council showcases accomplished researchers, influential educators shaping the next generation of project managers and recognised authorities on modern project management. In October 2011 he was awarded a prestigious Honorary Fellowship from the Association for Project Management for outstanding contribution to project management.

He has delivered lectures and courses in many international institutions, including King's College London, Cranfield Business School, ESC Lille, Iceland University, University of Southern Denmark, and George Washington University. His research interests include project success and failure; maturity and capability; ethics; process improvement; agile project management; systems and software engineering; project benchmarking; risk management; decision making; chaos and complexity; project leadership; change management; knowledge management; evidence-based and reflective practice.

Professor Dalcher is an Honorary Fellow of the Association for Project Management, a Chartered Fellow of the British Computer Society, a Fellow of the Chartered Management Institute, and the Royal Society of Arts, and a Member of the Project Management Institute, the Academy of Management, the Institute for Electrical and Electronics Engineers, and the Association for Computing Machinery. He is a Chartered IT Practitioner. He is a Member of the PMI Advisory Board responsible for the prestigious David I. Cleland Project Management Award; of the APM Group Ethics and Standards Governance Board, and, until recently; of the APM Professional Development Board. He is a member of the OGC's International Reference Group for Managing Successful Programmes; and Academic and Editorial Advisory Council Member for PM Today, for which he also writes a regular column featuring advances in research and practice in project management.

National Centre for Project Management
University of Hertfordshire
MacLaurin Building
4 Bishops Square
Hatfield, Herts.
AL10 9NE
Email: ncpm@herts.ac.uk